Mediterranean Refresh Cookbook 2021

500-Day Quick & Easy Healthy Recipes that Busy and Novice Can Cook Living and Eating Well Every Day on the Mediterranean Diet

Sedry Ramos

Table of contents

Introduction

The Mediterranean Refresh diet isn't trendy—it's been around for centuries. It's still popular today due to its abundance of healthy ingredients, fresh flavors, and simplicity in preparing. The Mediterranean Refresh Cookbook 2021 is your guide to easily incorporating this lifestyle to make tasty meals any time of the day.

People who follow the Mediterranean Refresh diet have a longer life expectancy and lower rates of chronic diseases than do other adults. The authentic Mediterranean Refresh diet is not only healthy, but also delicious! The Mediterranean Refresh Cookbook 2021 is the only resource you'll need.

The purpose of this book was to take this amazing way to provide healthy Mediterranean Refresh meal options! A huge range of delicious meal ideas will keep you and your family happy and well-fed, with fresh and tasty ingredients everybody will love.

Chapter 1: Overview

Mediterranean diet is not just a diet plan it is one of the healthy eating lifestyles. Most of the scientific study and research conducted over the Mediterranean diet proves that the Mediterranean diet helps to reduce your excess weight, cancer cell reduction and also reduces the risk of cardiovascular diseases.

Most of the scientific study also proves that the food consumption during the Mediterranean diet like vegetables, whole grain, nuts, fish and seasonable fruits improves blood vessels functions and reduce the risk of metabolic syndrome.

What is the Mediterranean diet?

Mediterranean diet is one of the traditional diets comes from different Mediterranean countries and regions. Mediterranean diet is basically a plant-based diet that allows you high consumption of vegetables, fruits, nuts, beans, grains, fish and olive oil. Mediterranean diet is a rich fat diet, it allows near about 40 percent of calories from fat. It also allows for consuming a moderate amount of protein and low consumption of meat and dairy products.

Mediterranean diet linked with good health and a healthier heart, it helps to reduce your health issues like diabetes and heart-related disease.

The history of the Mediterranean diet?

Mediterranean diet is one of the oldest diets plans popular in worldwide. It is near about more than three thousand years old diet plan. Mediterranean is the name of the sea situated between Asia, Europe and Africa. Mediterranean diet is an eating habit of people's lives around the coast of the Mediterranean Sea like Italy, France, Spain, Greece and Morocco. There are near about 22 countries situated near the Mediterranean Sea. The large amounts of seasonable fruits are available during four seasons because of mild climate.

There are large numbers of olive trees found in Mediterranean regions. Near about 90 percent of the world, olive trees are grown in Mediterranean regions. Due to large sea coast fishing is the main occupation by most of the people in this region and fish is part of the

Mediterranean diet. Most of the scientific study conducted over Mediterranean diet proves that the diet helps to reduce the all-cause mortality. It also reduces the risk of heart-related disease and early death.

The Science Behind Mediterranean diet

Mediterranean diet is one of the high-fat diets that allow near about 40 percent of calories from fat. It is the most studied and healthiest diet worldwide.

The scientific research and study show that the peoples who follow the Mediterranean diet have lower the risk of cardiac mortality and heart disease. The study shows that the Mediterranean diet is a high-fat diet; during the diet, our body consumes a high intake of unsaturated fat and low intake of saturated fat. Unsaturated fats help to increase the HDL (Good Cholesterol) level into your body. Olive oil is one of the main fats used during the Mediterranean diet. Olive oils are full of monounsaturated fats that help to control your diabetes. It improves your insulin sensitivity and controls your diabetes. If you don't have diabetes then it helps to reduce the risk of developing diabetes.

Another study shows that the Mediterranean diet reduces the risk of stomach cancer and also reducing the risk of breast cancer in women.

Benefits of the Mediterranean diet

Mediterranean diet is one of the oldest diets in the world comes with various types of health benefits. Some of the important benefits are as follows.

- **Improves heart health**

During the Mediterranean diet, olive oil is used as a primary fat. This olive oil contains healthy fat known as monounsaturated fat helps to increase the HDL (Good Cholesterol) level and reduce the LDL (Bad Cholesterol) level. Fish is also part of the Mediterranean lifestyle, fish contains Omega-3 fatty acid which helps to improve the heart health and reduce the risk of heart failure, strokes, and sudden cardiac death.

- **Help to maintain blood sugar level**

According to the American Heart Association, the Mediterranean diet is low in sugar. It is very effective in type-2 diabetes patients and helps to maintain the blood sugar level. Mediterranean diet is rich in monounsaturated fats which help to reduce the cholesterol level and maintain your blood sugar level.

- **Increase your lifespan**

Mediterranean region's climate is clear and pollution-free climate. Due to this, you have to find fresh vegetables, seasonable fruits, beans, olives and fish in this region. All of the natural and fresh foods are full of antioxidants, which helps to reduce the inflammation in your body and slow down your aging process. It also reduces the risk of heart-related disease, inflammation, Alzheimer's and depression. The peoples live in Mediterranean regions have a longer lifespan.

- **Protects from cancer**

Mediterranean diet is one of the simple plant-based food diet. It allows high fat moderate protein and low consumption of red meat. Most of the scientific study and research show that reduction of red meat from your diet and increase the consumption of olive oil and fish into your daily diet will help to reduce the risk of several common cancers. Fish contains omega-3 fatty acids which reduce the risk of cancer.

- **Fight against depression**

The foods associated with the Mediterranean diet have anti-inflammatory properties which help to reduce the depression and help to improve your mood. One of the scientific research studies shows that the peoples who follow the Mediterranean diet have 98.6 percent of lower the risk of depression.

Chapter 2: Breakfast & Brunch

Vegetable Quinoa

Preparation Time: 10 minutes

Cooking Time: 1 minute

Serve: 6

Ingredients:

- 1 cup quinoa, rinsed and drained
- 1 1/2 cups water
- 4 cups spinach, chopped
- 1 bell pepper, chopped
- 2 carrots, chopped
- 1 celery stalk, chopped
- 1/3 cup feta cheese, crumbled
- 1/2 cup olives, sliced
- 1/3 cup pesto
- 2 tomatoes, chopped
- Pepper
- Salt

Directions:

1. Add quinoa, spinach, bell pepper, carrots, celery, water, pepper, and salt into the instant pot and stir well.
2. Seal pot with lid and cook on high for 1 minute.
3. Once done, allow to release pressure naturally for 10 minutes then release remaining using quick release. Remove lid.
4. Add remaining ingredients and stir everything well.
5. Serve and enjoy.

Nutritional Value (Amount per Serving):

- Calories 226
- Fat 10.7 g
- Carbohydrates 26 g
- Sugar 4.4 g
- Protein 7.9 g
- Cholesterol 11 mg

Almond Peach Oatmeal

Preparation Time: 10 minutes

Cooking Time: 10 minutes

Serve: 2

Ingredients:

- 1 cup unsweetened almond milk
- 2 cups of water
- 1 cup oats
- 2 peaches, diced
- Pinch of salt

Directions:

1. Spray instant pot from inside with cooking spray.
2. Add all ingredients into the instant pot and stir well.
3. Seal pot with a lid and select manual and set timer for 10 minutes.
4. Once done, allow to release pressure naturally for 10 minutes then release remaining using quick release. Remove lid.
5. Stir and serve.

Nutritional Value (Amount per Serving):

- Calories 234
- Fat 4.8 g
- Carbohydrates 42.7 g
- Sugar 6.9 g
- Protein 7.3 g
- Cholesterol 0 mg

Mushroom Cheese Breakfast

Preparation Time: 10 minutes

Cooking Time: 12 minutes

Serve: 4

Ingredients:

- 5 eggs
- 2 tbsp olive oil
- 1 onion, chopped
- 2 tbsp chives, minced
- 1 1/2 cups mushrooms, sliced
- 1/2 cup almond milk
- 1/2 tbsp cheddar cheese
- 1 bell pepper, chopped
- Pepper
- Salt

Directions:

1. Add oil into the instant pot and set the pot on sauté mode.
2. Add mushrooms and sauté for 2 minutes. Transfer mushrooms on a plate and clean the instant pot.
3. In a bowl, whisk eggs with pepper and salt. Add mushrooms, onion, chives, almond milk, cheese, and bell pepper into the egg mixture and whisk well.
4. Spray baking dish with cooking spray.
5. Pour 1 1/2 cups of water into the instant pot then place steamer rack in the pot.
6. Pour egg mixture into the prepared baking dish. Cover dish with foil.
7. Place baking dish on top of the steamer rack.
8. Seal pot with lid and cook on high for 10 minutes.
9. Once done, release pressure using quick release. Remove lid.
10. Serve and enjoy.

Nutritional Value (Amount per Serving):

- Calories 238
- Fat 20.1 g
- Carbohydrates 7.9 g
- Sugar 4.6 g
- Protein 9.3 g
- Cholesterol 206 mg

Date Apple Oats

Preparation Time: 10 minutes

Cooking Time: 4 minutes

Serve: 2

Ingredients:

- 1/4 cup oats
- 1/4 tsp vanilla
- 14 tsp cinnamon
- 2 dates, chopped
- 1 apple, chopped
- 1/2 cup water

Directions:

1. Spray instant pot from inside with cooking spray.
2. Add all ingredients to the instant pot and stir well.
3. Seal pot with lid and cook on high for 4 minutes.
4. Once done, allow to release pressure naturally for 10 minutes then release remaining using quick release. Remove lid.
5. Stir well and serve.

Nutritional Value (Amount per Serving):

- Calories 161
- Fat 1.1 g
- Carbohydrates 41.6 g
- Sugar 17.4 g
- Protein 2.5 g
- Cholesterol 0 mg

Quinoa Breakfast Bowls

Preparation Time: 10 minutes

Cooking Time: 4 minutes

Serve: 4

Ingredients:

- 1 cup quinoa, rinsed and drained
- 1 cucumber, chopped
- 1 red bell pepper, chopped
- 1/2 cup olives, pitted and sliced
- 1 tbsp fresh basil, chopped
- 2 tbsp fresh lemon juice
- 1 tsp lemon zest, grated
- 1 1/2 cups water
- Pepper
- Salt

Directions:

1. Add quinoa, lemon zest, lemon juice, water, pepper, and salt into the instant pot and stir well.
2. Seal pot with lid and cook on high for 4 minutes.
3. Once done, allow to release pressure naturally for 10 minutes then release remaining using quick release. Remove lid.
4. Add remaining ingredients and stir well.
5. Serve immediately and enjoy it.

Nutritional Value (Amount per Serving):

- Calories 199
- Fat 4.6 g
- Carbohydrates 33.6 g
- Sugar 3 g
- Protein 7 g
- Cholesterol 0 mg

Simple Lemon Quinoa

Preparation Time: 10 minutes

Cooking Time: 1 minute

Serve: 4

Ingredients:

- 2 cups quinoa, rinsed and drained
- 1 fresh lemon juice
- 2 tbsp fresh parsley, chopped
- 3 cups of water
- 1/4 tsp salt

Directions:

1. Spray instant pot from inside with cooking spray.
2. Add all ingredients except lemon juice and parsley into the pot. Stir well.
3. Seal pot with lid and cook on high for 1 minute.
4. Once done, allow to release pressure naturally for 10 minutes then release remaining using quick release. Remove lid.
5. Add parsley and lemon juice.
6. Stir and serve.

Nutritional Value (Amount per Serving):

- Calories 317
- Fat 5.3 g
- Carbohydrates 54.9 g
- Sugar 0.3 g
- Protein 12.2 g
- Cholesterol 0 mg

Breakfast Cauliflower Rice Bowl

Preparation Time: 10 minutes

Cooking Time: 12 minutes

Serve: 6

Ingredients:

- 1 cup cauliflower rice
- 1/2 tsp red pepper flakes
- 1 1/2 tsp curry powder
- 1/2 tbsp ginger, grated
- 1 cup vegetable stock
- 4 tomatoes, chopped
- 3 cups broccoli, chopped
- Pepper
- Salt

Directions:

1. Spray instant pot from inside with cooking spray.
2. Add all ingredients into the instant pot and stir well.
3. Seal pot with lid and cook on high for 12 minutes.
4. Once done, allow to release pressure naturally for 10 minutes then release remaining using quick release. Remove lid.
5. Stir and serve.

Nutritional Value (Amount per Serving):

- Calories 44
- Fat 0.8 g
- Carbohydrates 8.2 g
- Sugar 3.8 g
- Protein 2.8 g
- Cholesterol 0 mg

Pear Breakfast Rice

Preparation Time: 10 minutes

Cooking Time: 15 minutes

Serve: 4

Ingredients:

- 1 1/2 cups rice
- 3 cups almond milk
- 2 pears, cored and sliced
- 2 tbsp maple syrup
- 1 tsp ground cinnamon

Directions:

1. Spray instant pot from inside with cooking spray.
2. Set instant pot on sauté mode. Add rice and sauté for 5 minutes.
3. Add remaining ingredients except for maple syrup and stir well.
4. Seal pot with lid and cook on high for 10 minutes.
5. Once done, allow to release pressure naturally for 10 minutes then release remaining using quick release. Remove lid.
6. Stir in maple syrup and serve.

Nutritional Value (Amount per Serving):

- Calories 755
- Fat 43.6 g
- Carbohydrates 88.5 g
- Sugar 22.2 g
- Protein 9.5 g
- Cholesterol 0 mg

Healthy Buckwheat Porridge

Preparation Time: 10 minutes

Cooking Time: 6 minutes

Serve: 2

Ingredients:

- 1 cup buckwheat groats, rinsed
- 1 tsp ground cinnamon
- 1 banana, sliced
- 3 cups unsweetened almond milk
- Pinch of salt

Directions:

1. Spray instant pot from inside with cooking spray.
2. Add all ingredients into the instant pot and stir well.
3. Seal pot with lid and cook on high for 6 minutes.
4. Once done, release pressure using quick release. Remove lid.
5. Stir and serve.

Nutritional Value (Amount per Serving):

- Calories 316
- Fat 7.3 g
- Carbohydrates 59.8 g
- Sugar 8.8 g
- Protein 9.8 g
- Cholesterol 0 mg

Buckwheat Breakfast Bowls

Preparation Time: 10 minutes

Cooking Time: 15 minutes

Serve: 4

Ingredients:

- 1 cup buckwheat
- 1 tsp ground cinnamon
- 1 tbsp almonds, chopped
- 1 tbsp walnuts, chopped
- 1 cup heavy cream
- 2 cups almond milk

Directions:

1. Spray instant pot from inside with cooking spray.
2. Add all ingredients into the instant pot and stir well.
3. Seal pot with lid and cook on high for 15 minutes.
4. Once done, allow to release pressure naturally for 10 minutes then release remaining using quick release. Remove lid.
5. Stir and serve.

Nutritional Value (Amount per Serving):

- Calories 547
- Fat 43.1 g
- Carbohydrates 38.9 g
- Sugar 4.1 g
- Protein 9.8 g
- Cholesterol 41 mg

Chapter 3: Soups & Stews

Simple Black Bean Soup

Preparation Time: 10 minutes

Cooking Time: 40 minutes

Serve: 8

Ingredients:

- 1 lb black beans, soaked overnight
- 1 tbsp olive oil
- 1 tbsp fresh parsley, chopped
- 1 onion, chopped
- 7 cups vegetable stock
- 2 tbsp vinegar
- Pepper
- Salt

Directions:

1. Add all ingredients except parsley and vinegar into the instant pot and stir well.
2. Seal pot with lid and cook on high pressure 40 for minutes.
3. Once done, allow to release pressure naturally for 10 minutes then release remaining using quick release. Remove lid.
4. Stir in parsley and vinegar and serve.

Nutritional Value (Amount per Serving):

- Calories 220
- Fat 2.7 g
- Carbohydrates 37.5 g
- Sugar 2.4 g
- Protein 12.8 g
- Cholesterol 0 mg

Cheese Kale Soup

Preparation Time: 10 minutes

Cooking Time: 5 minutes

Serve: 4

Ingredients:

- 6 cups fresh kale, chopped
- 1 tbsp olive oil
- 3/4 cup cottage cheese, cut into chunks
- 3 cups vegetable broth
- Pepper
- salt

Directions:

1. Add all ingredients except cheese into the instant pot and stir well.
2. Seal pot with lid and cook on high for 5 minutes.
3. Once done, release pressure using quick release. Remove lid.
4. Stir in cottage cheese and serve.

Nutritional Value (Amount per Serving):

- Calories 147
- Fat 5.4 g
- Carbohydrates 12.7 g
- Sugar 0.7 g
- Protein 12.5 g
- Cholesterol 3 mg

Delicious Okra Chicken Stew

Preparation Time: 10 minutes

Cooking Time: 20 minutes

Serve: 4

Ingredients:

- 1 lb chicken breasts, skinless, boneless, and cubed
- 1 lemon juice
- 1/4 cup fresh parsley, chopped
- 1 tbsp olive oil
- 12 oz can tomatoes, crushed
- 1 tsp allspice
- 14 oz okra, chopped
- 2 cups chicken stock
- 1 tsp garlic, minced
- 1 onion, chopped
- Pepper
- Salt

Directions:

1. Add oil into the inner pot of instant pot and set the pot on sauté mode.
2. Add chicken and onion and sauté until chicken is lightly brown about 5 minutes.
3. Add remaining ingredients except for the parsley and stir well.
4. Seal pot with lid and cook on high pressure 15 for minutes.
5. Once done, allow to release pressure naturally for 10 minutes then release remaining using quick release. Remove lid.
6. Stir well and serve.

Nutritional Value (Amount per Serving):

- Calories 326
- Fat 12.6 g
- Carbohydrates 15.8 g
- Sugar 6.2 g
- Protein 36.4 g
- Cholesterol 101 mg

Cheesy Chicken Soup

Preparation Time: 10 minutes

Cooking Time: 15 minutes

Serve: 4

Ingredients:

- 12 oz chicken thighs, boneless
- 1 cup heavy cream
- 2 cups cheddar cheese, shredded
- 3 cups chicken stock
- 2 tbsp olive oil
- 1/2 cup celery, chopped
- 1/4 cup hot sauce
- 1 tsp garlic, minced
- 1/4 cup onion, chopped

Directions:

1. Add all ingredients except cream and cheese into the instant pot and stir well.
2. Seal pot with lid and cook on high pressure 15 for minutes.
3. Once done, allow to release pressure naturally. Remove lid.
4. Shred the chicken using a fork.
5. Add cream and cheese and stir until cheese is melted.
6. Serve and enjoy.

Nutritional Value (Amount per Serving):

- Calories 568
- Fat 43.6 g
- Carbohydrates 3.6 g
- Sugar 1.5 g
- Protein 40.1 g
- Cholesterol 176 mg

Roasted Tomatoes Soup

Preparation Time: 10 minutes

Cooking Time: 5 minutes

Serve: 2

Ingredients:

- 14 oz can fire-roasted tomatoes
- 1 1/2 cups vegetable stock
- 1/4 cup zucchini, grated
- 1/2 tsp dried oregano
- 1/2 tsp dried basil
- 1/2 cup heavy cream
- 1/2 cup parmesan cheese, grated
- 1 cup cheddar cheese, grated
- Pepper
- Salt

Directions:

1. Add tomatoes, stock, zucchini, oregano, basil, pepper, and salt into the instant pot and stir well.
2. Seal pot with lid and cook on high for 5 minutes.
3. Once done, release pressure using quick release. Remove lid.
4. Set pot on sauté mode. Add heavy cream, parmesan cheese, and cheddar cheese and stir well and cook until cheese is melted.
5. Serve and enjoy.

Nutritional Value (Amount per Serving):

- Calories 460
- Fat 34.8 g
- Carbohydrates 13.5 g
- Sugar 6 g
- Protein 24.1 g
- Cholesterol 117 mg

Curried Zucchini Soup

Preparation Time: 10 minutes

Cooking Time: 10 minutes

Serve: 6

Ingredients:

- 10 cups zucchini, chopped
- 4 cups vegetable broth
- 14 oz coconut milk
- 1 tsp curry powder
- Pepper
- Salt

Directions:

1. Add all ingredients into the instant pot and stir well.
2. Seal pot with lid and cook on high for 10 minutes.
3. Once done, release pressure using quick release. Remove lid.
4. Blend soup using an immersion blender until smooth.
5. Serve and enjoy.

Nutritional Value (Amount per Serving):

- Calories 209
- Fat 17.1 g
- Carbohydrates 10.8 g
- Sugar 5.9 g
- Protein 7.1 g
- Cholesterol 0 mg

Creamy Potato Soup

Preparation Time: 10 minutes

Cooking Time: 10 minutes

Serve: 4

Ingredients:

- 3/4 lb potato, peeled and diced
- 2 leeks, sliced
- 4 cups vegetable stock
- 1 tsp garlic, minced
- 1 onion, chopped
- 1 tbsp olive oil
- Pepper
- Salt

Directions:

1. Add oil into the inner pot of instant pot and set the pot on sauté mode.
2. Add onion and sauté for 2 minutes.
3. Add garlic and leek and sauté for 2 minutes.
4. Add remaining ingredients and stir well.
5. Seal pot with lid and cook on high for 6 minutes.
6. Once done, allow to release pressure naturally for 10 minutes then release remaining using quick release. Remove lid.
7. Blend soup using an immersion blender until smooth.
8. Serve and enjoy.

Nutritional Value (Amount per Serving):

- Calories 141
- Fat 3.8 g
- Carbohydrates 24.9 g
- Sugar 4.3 g
- Protein 3.1 g
- Cholesterol 0 mg

Easy Cauliflower Soup

Preparation Time: 10 minutes

Cooking Time: 30 minutes

Serve: 4

Ingredients:

- 2 cups cauliflower florets
- 3 tbsp olive oil
- 1 onion, chopped
- 1 tsp pumpkin pie spice
- 5 cups chicken broth
- 1/4 tsp salt

Directions:

1. Add oil into the inner pot of instant pot and set the pot on sauté mode.
2. Add onion and sauté for 5 minutes.
3. Add remaining ingredients and stir well.
4. Seal pot with lid and cook on high for 25 minutes.
5. Once done, release pressure using quick release. Remove lid.
6. Blend soup using an immersion blender until smooth.
7. Serve and enjoy.

Nutritional Value (Amount per Serving):

- Calories 163
- Fat 12.3 g
- Carbohydrates 6.7 g
- Sugar 3.3 g
- Protein 6.6 g
- Cholesterol 0 mg

Healthy Vegetable Soup

Preparation Time: 10 minutes

Cooking Time: 15 minutes

Serve: 4

Ingredients:

- 1 cup can tomatoes, chopped
- 1 small zucchini, diced
- 3 oz kale, sliced
- 1 tbsp garlic, chopped
- 5 button mushrooms, sliced
- 2 carrots, peeled and sliced
- 2 celery sticks, sliced
- 1/2 red chili, sliced
- 1 onion, diced
- 1 tbsp olive oil
- 1 bay leaf
- 4 cups vegetable stock
- 1/4 tsp salt

Directions:

1. Add oil into the inner pot of instant pot and set the pot on sauté mode.
2. Add carrots, celery, onion, and salt and cook for 2-3 minutes.
3. Add mushrooms and chili and cook for 2 minutes.
4. Add remaining ingredients and stir everything well.
5. Seal pot with lid and cook on high for 10 minutes.
6. Once done, allow to release pressure naturally for 10 minutes then release remaining using quick release. Remove lid.
7. Stir well and serve.

Nutritional Value (Amount per Serving):

- Calories 100
- Fat 3.8 g
- Carbohydrates 15.1 g
- Sugar 6.6 g
- Protein 3.5 g
- Cholesterol 0 mg

Celery Soup

Preparation Time: 10 minutes

Cooking Time: 30 minutes

Serve: 4

Ingredients:

- 6 cups celery stalk, chopped
- 1 cup heavy cream
- 1 onion, chopped
- 2 cups vegetable broth
- 1/2 tsp dill
- Salt

Directions:

1. Add all ingredients into the instant pot and stir well.
2. Seal pot with lid and cook on high for 30 minutes.
3. Once done, release pressure using quick release. Remove lid.
4. Blend soup using an immersion blender until smooth.
5. Serve and enjoy.

Nutritional Value (Amount per Serving):

- Calories 158
- Fat 12.1 g
- Carbohydrates 8.4 g
- Sugar 3.6 g
- Protein 4.4 g
- Cholesterol 41 mg

Chapter 4: Pasta, Grains & Beans

Flavors Taco Rice Bowl

Preparation Time: 10 minutes

Cooking Time: 14 minutes

Serve: 8

Ingredients:

- 1 lb ground beef
- 8 oz cheddar cheese, shredded
- 14 oz can red beans
- 2 oz taco seasoning
- 16 oz salsa
- 2 cups of water
- 2 cups brown rice
- Pepper
- Salt

Directions:

1. Set instant pot on sauté mode.
2. Add meat to the pot and sauté until brown.
3. Add water, beans, rice, taco seasoning, pepper, and salt and stir well.
4. Top with salsa. Seal pot with lid and cook on high for 14 minutes.
5. Once done, release pressure using quick release. Remove lid.
6. Add cheddar cheese and stir until cheese is melted.
7. Serve and enjoy.

Nutritional Value (Amount per Serving):

- Calories 464
- Fat 15.3 g
- Carbohydrates 48.9 g
- Sugar 2.8 g
- Protein 32.2 g
- Cholesterol 83 mg

Fiber Packed Chicken Rice

Preparation Time: 10 minutes

Cooking Time: 16 minutes

Serve: 6

Ingredients:

- 1 lb chicken breast, skinless, boneless, and cut into chunks
- 14.5 oz can cannellini beans
- 4 cups chicken broth
- 2 cups wild rice
- 1 tbsp Italian seasoning
- 1 small onion, chopped
- 1 tbsp garlic, chopped
- 1 tbsp olive oil
- Pepper
- Salt

Directions:

1. Add oil into the inner pot of instant pot and set the pot on sauté mode.
2. Add garlic and onion and sauté for 2 minutes.
3. Add chicken and cook for 2 minutes.
4. Add remaining ingredients and stir well.
5. Seal pot with lid and cook on high for 12 minutes.
6. Once done, release pressure using quick release. Remove lid.
7. Stir well and serve.

Nutritional Value (Amount per Serving):

- Calories 399
- Fat 6.4 g
- Carbohydrates 53.4 g
- Sugar 3 g
- Protein 31.6 g
- Cholesterol 50 mg

Cheese Basil Tomato Rice

Preparation Time: 10 minutes

Cooking Time: 26 minutes

Serve: 8

Ingredients:

- 1 1/2 cups brown rice
- 1 cup parmesan cheese, grated
- 1/4 cup fresh basil, chopped
- 2 cups grape tomatoes, halved
- 8 oz can tomato sauce
- 1 3/4 cup vegetable broth
- 1 tbsp garlic, minced
- 1/2 cup onion, diced
- 1 tbsp olive oil
- Pepper
- Salt

Directions:

1. Add oil into the inner pot of instant pot and set the pot on sauté mode.
2. Add garlic and onion and sauté for 4 minutes.
3. Add rice, tomato sauce, broth, pepper, and salt and stir well.
4. Seal pot with lid and cook on high for 22 minutes.
5. Once done, allow to release pressure naturally for 10 minutes then release remaining using quick release. Remove lid.
6. Add remaining ingredients and stir well.
7. Serve and enjoy.

Nutritional Value (Amount per Serving):

- Calories 208
- Fat 5.6 g
- Carbohydrates 32.1 g
- Sugar 2.8 g
- Protein 8.3 g
- Cholesterol 8 mg

Spinach Pesto Pasta

Preparation Time: 10 minutes

Cooking Time: 10 minutes

Serve: 4

Ingredients:

- 8 oz whole-grain pasta
- 1/3 cup mozzarella cheese, grated
- 1/2 cup pesto
- 5 oz fresh spinach
- 1 3/4 cup water
- 8 oz mushrooms, chopped
- 1 tbsp olive oil
- Pepper
- Salt

Directions:

1. Add oil into the inner pot of instant pot and set the pot on sauté mode.
2. Add mushrooms and sauté for 5 minutes.
3. Add water and pasta and stir well.
4. Seal pot with lid and cook on high for 5 minutes.
5. Once done, release pressure using quick release. Remove lid.
6. Stir in remaining ingredients and serve.

Nutritional Value (Amount per Serving):

- Calories 213
- Fat 17.3 g
- Carbohydrates 9.5 g
- Sugar 4.5 g
- Protein 7.4 g
- Cholesterol 9 mg

Classic Greek Lentils & Rice

Preparation Time: 10 minutes

Cooking Time: 16 minutes

Serve: 6

Ingredients:

- 1/3 cup lentils, soak for 1-2 hours
- 2 cups vegetable stock
- 1/2 tsp ground coriander
- 1/4 tsp ground cumin
- 1 cup of brown rice
- 2 tbsp olive oil
- 2 cups onion, sliced
- Salt

Directions:

1. Add oil into the inner pot of instant pot and set the pot on sauté mode.
2. Add onion and sauté for 5-10 minutes.
3. Add the rest of the ingredients and stir well.
4. Seal pot with lid and cook on high for 6 minutes.
5. Once done, allow to release pressure naturally for 10 minutes then release remaining using quick release. Remove lid.
6. Serve and enjoy.

Nutritional Value (Amount per Serving):

- Calories 210
- Fat 5.7 g
- Carbohydrates 34.5 g
- Sugar 2.1 g
- Protein 5.7 g
- Cholesterol 0 mg

Garlic Zucchini Rice

Preparation Time: 10 minutes

Cooking Time: 13 minutes

Serve: 4

Ingredients:

- 12 oz rice
- 1/2 tsp allspice
- 1 tsp thyme, chopped
- 1 zucchini, grated
- 4 cups vegetable stock
- 1 tsp garlic, minced
- 1 onion, chopped
- 2 tbsp olive oil
- Pepper
- Salt

Directions:

1. Add oil into the inner pot of instant pot and set the pot on sauté mode.
2. Add garlic and sauté for 1 minute.
3. Add remaining ingredients and stir well.
4. Seal pot with lid and cook on high for 12 minutes.
5. Once done, allow to release pressure naturally for 5 minutes then release remaining using quick release. Remove lid.
6. Serve and enjoy.

Nutritional Value (Amount per Serving):

- Calories 398
- Fat 7.8 g
- Carbohydrates 73.7 g
- Sugar 2.8 g
- Protein 7.4 g
- Cholesterol 0 mg

Corn Risotto

Preparation Time: 10 minutes

Cooking Time: 12 minutes

Serve: 4

Ingredients:

- 1 cup of rice
- 3 cups vegetable broth
- 1 tbsp olive oil
- 1 tsp garlic, minced
- 1 onion, chopped
- 3/4 cup sweet corn
- 1 red pepper, diced
- 1 tsp dried mix herbs
- 1/4 tsp pepper
- 1/2 tsp salt

Directions:

1. Add oil into the inner pot of instant pot and set the pot on sauté mode.
2. Add onion and garlic and sauté for 5 minutes.
3. Add the rest of the ingredients and stir well.
4. Seal pot with lid and cook on high for 8 minutes.
5. Once done, release pressure using quick release. Remove lid.
6. Stir well and serve.

Nutritional Value (Amount per Serving):

- Calories 304
- Fat 5.3 g
- Carbohydrates 54.5 g
- Sugar 4.7 g
- Protein 9.5 g
- Cholesterol 0 mg

Kidney Bean Salad

Preparation Time: 10 minutes

Cooking Time: 17 minutes

Serve: 4

Ingredients:

- 1 lb dry kidney beans, soaked overnight
- 2 tbsp fresh parsley, chopped
- 2 tbsp green onion, minced
- 1 1/2 cups vegetable stock
- 1 tsp dried thyme
- 1 red bell pepper, chopped
- 1 tbsp garlic, chopped
- 1 onion, chopped
- 1 tsp olive oil
- Pepper
- Salt

Directions:

1. Add oil into the inner pot of instant pot and set the pot on sauté mode.
2. Add garlic and onion and sauté for 2 minutes.
3. Add remaining ingredients and stir well.
4. Seal pot with lid and cook on high for 15 minutes.
5. Once done, allow to release pressure naturally for 10 minutes then release remaining using quick release. Remove lid.
6. Stir well and serve.

Nutritional Value (Amount per Serving):

- Calories 420
- Fat 2.6 g
- Carbohydrates 75.9 g
- Sugar 5.4 g
- Protein 26.6 g
- Cholesterol 0 mg

Brown Rice Pilaf

Preparation Time: 10 minutes

Cooking Time: 27 minutes

Serve: 6

Ingredients:

- 1 1/2 cups brown rice, rinsed and drained
- 2 tbsp parsley, chopped
- 1 3/4 cups vegetable broth
- 1 tsp garlic, minced
- 1/2 cup onion, diced
- 2 tbsp olive oil
- 1/2 tsp salt

Directions:

1. Add oil into the inner pot of instant pot and set the pot on sauté mode.
2. Add onion and sauté for 5 minutes.
3. Add the rest of the ingredients except parsley and stir well.
4. Seal pot with lid and cook on high for 22 minutes.
5. Once done, allow to release pressure naturally. Remove lid.
6. Garnish with parsley and serve.

Nutritional Value (Amount per Serving):

- Calories 228
- Fat 6.4 g
- Carbohydrates 37.6 g
- Sugar 0.6 g
- Protein 5.2 g
- Cholesterol 0 mg

Delicious Chicken Pasta

Preparation Time: 10 minutes

Cooking Time: 17 minutes

Serve: 4

Ingredients:

- 3 chicken breasts, skinless, boneless, cut into pieces
- 9 oz whole-grain pasta
- 1/2 cup olives, sliced
- 1/2 cup sun-dried tomatoes
- 1 tbsp roasted red peppers, chopped
- 14 oz can tomatoes, diced
- 2 cups marinara sauce
- 1 cup chicken broth
- Pepper
- Salt

Directions:

1. Add all ingredients except whole-grain pasta into the instant pot and stir well.
2. Seal pot with lid and cook on high for 12 minutes.
3. Once done, allow to release pressure naturally. Remove lid.
4. Add pasta and stir well. Seal pot again and select manual and set timer for 5 minutes.
5. Once done, allow to release pressure naturally for 5 minutes then release remaining using quick release. Remove lid.
6. Stir well and serve.

Nutritional Value (Amount per Serving):

- Calories 615
- Fat 15.4 g
- Carbohydrates 71 g
- Sugar 17.6 g
- Protein 48 g
- Cholesterol 100 mg

Chapter 5: Vegetables

Garlic Parmesan Artichokes

Preparation Time: 10 minutes

Cooking Time: 10 minutes

Serve: 4

Ingredients:

- 4 artichokes, wash, trim, and cut top
- 1/2 cup vegetable broth
- 1/4 cup parmesan cheese, grated
- 1 tbsp olive oil
- 2 tsp garlic, minced
- Salt

Directions:

1. Pour broth into the instant pot then place steamer rack in the pot.
2. Place artichoke steam side down on steamer rack into the pot.
3. Sprinkle garlic and grated cheese on top of artichokes and season with salt. Drizzle oil over artichokes.
4. Seal pot with lid and cook on high for 10 minutes.
5. Once done, release pressure using quick release. Remove lid.
6. Serve and enjoy.

Nutritional Value (Amount per Serving):

- Calories 132
- Fat 5.2 g
- Carbohydrates 17.8 g
- Sugar 1.7 g
- Protein 7.9 g
- Cholesterol 4 mg

Spicy Mushrooms

Preparation Time: 10 minutes

Cooking Time: 5 minutes

Serve: 4

Ingredients:

- 1 lb mushrooms, sliced
- 1 tbsp fresh lemon juice
- 1 tbsp balsamic vinegar
- 1/4 tsp paprika
- 1/4 tsp ground cumin
- 1/4 tsp dried oregano
- 1 chipotle chili in adobo sauce
- 1 tbsp garlic, minced
- 2 tbsp olive oil
- Salt

Directions:

1. Add oil into the inner pot of instant pot and set the pot on sauté mode.
2. Add garlic and mushrooms and sauté for 2 minutes.
3. Add remaining ingredients and stir everything well.
4. Seal pot with lid and cook on high for 3 minutes.
5. Once done, release pressure using quick release. Remove lid.
6. Stir well and serve.

Nutritional Value (Amount per Serving):

- Calories 97
- Fat 7.7 g
- Carbohydrates 5.5 g
- Sugar 2.6 g
- Protein 3.8 g
- Cholesterol 0 mg

Tomato & Cheese Mix

Preparation Time: 10 minutes

Cooking Time: 15 minutes

Serve: 4

Ingredients:

- 1 lb grape tomatoes, halved
- 1 cup feta cheese, crumbled
- 1 cup heavy cream
- 1 onion, chopped
- 1 tbsp olive oil
- 1/4 tsp Italian seasoning
- Pepper
- Salt

Directions:

1. Add oil into the inner pot of instant pot and set the pot on sauté mode.
2. Add onion and sauté for 3 minutes.
3. Add remaining ingredients and stir well.
4. Seal pot with lid and cook on high for 12 minutes.
5. Once done, release pressure using quick release. Remove lid.
6. Stir and serve.

Nutritional Value (Amount per Serving):

- Calories 265
- Fat 22.9 g
- Carbohydrates 9.4 g
- Sugar 5.7 g
- Protein 7.3 g
- Cholesterol 75 mg

Nutritious Potato Lentils

Preparation Time: 10 minutes

Cooking Time: 5 minutes

Serve: 2

Ingredients:

- 1 sweet potato, peeled and chopped
- 1/2 cup red lentils, rinsed and drained
- 1 1/2 cups water
- 2 tbsp vinegar
- 1/4 tsp chili powder
- 1/4 tsp garlic powder
- 1/4 tsp cinnamon
- 1 small onion, chopped

Directions:

1. Add all ingredients into the inner pot of instant pot and stir well.
2. Seal pot with lid and cook on high for 5 minutes.
3. Once done, allow to release pressure naturally for 10 minutes then release remaining using quick release. Remove lid.
4. Serve over cooked brown rice.

Nutritional Value (Amount per Serving):

- Calories 241
- Fat 0.7 g
- Carbohydrates 44.7 g
- Sugar 6.3 g
- Protein 14 g
- Cholesterol 0 mg

Potato Salad

Preparation Time: 10 minutes

Cooking Time: 10 minutes

Serve: 8

Ingredients:

- 5 cups potato, cubed
- 1/4 cup fresh parsley, chopped
- 1/4 tsp red pepper flakes
- 1 tbsp olive oil
- 1/3 cup mayonnaise
- 1/2 tbsp oregano
- 2 tbsp capers
- 3/4 cup feta cheese, crumbled
- 1 cup olives, halved
- 3 cups of water
- 3/4 cup onion, chopped
- Pepper
- Salt

Directions:

1. Add potatoes, onion, and salt into the instant pot.
2. Seal pot with lid and cook on high for 3 minutes.
3. Once done, release pressure using quick release. Remove lid.
4. Remove potatoes from pot and place in a large mixing bowl.
5. Add remaining ingredients and stir everything well.
6. Serve and enjoy.

Nutritional Value (Amount per Serving):

- Calories 152
- Fat 9.9 g
- Carbohydrates 13.6 g
- Sugar 2.1 g
- Protein 3.5 g
- Cholesterol 15 mg

Creamy Dill Potatoes

Preparation Time: 10 minutes

Cooking Time: 20 minutes

Serve: 4

Ingredients:

- 2 lbs potatoes, peeled and cut into chunks
- 1 tbsp fresh dill, chopped
- 1 cup vegetable stock
- 3/4 cup heavy cream
- Pepper
- Salt

Directions:

1. Add all ingredients into the inner pot of instant pot and stir well.
2. Seal pot with lid and cook on high for 20 minutes.
3. Once done, allow to release pressure naturally for 10 minutes then release remaining using quick release. Remove lid.
4. Stir and serve.

Nutritional Value (Amount per Serving):

- Calories 238
- Fat 8.6 g
- Carbohydrates 37 g
- Sugar 2.8 g
- Protein 4.5 g
- Cholesterol 31 mg

Greek Green Beans

Preparation Time: 10 minutes
Cooking Time: 15 minutes
Serve: 4

Ingredients:

- 1 lb green beans, remove stems
- 2 potatoes, quartered
- 1 1/2 onion, sliced
- 1 tsp dried oregano
- 1/4 cup dill, chopped
- 1/4 cup fresh parsley, chopped
- 1 zucchini, quartered
- 1/2 cup olive oil
- 1 cup of water
- 14.5 oz can tomatoes, diced
- Pepper
- Salt

Directions:

1. Add all ingredients into the inner pot of instant pot and stir everything well.
2. Seal pot with lid and cook on high for 15 minutes.
3. Once done, release pressure using quick release. Remove lid.
4. Stir well and serve.

Nutritional Value (Amount per Serving):

- Calories 381
- Fat 25.8 g
- Carbohydrates 37.7 g
- Sugar 9 g
- Protein 6.6 g
- Cholesterol 0 mg

Zesty Green Beans

Preparation Time: 10 minutes

Cooking Time: 15 minutes

Serve: 4

Ingredients:

- 1 lb green beans, trimmed
- 1 cup vegetable stock
- 1 lemon juice
- 1 tsp lemon zest, grated
- Pepper
- Salt

Directions:

1. Pour the stock into the instant pot.
2. Add green beans, lemon juice, lemon zest, pepper, and salt into the bowl and toss well.
3. Transfer green beans into the steamer basket. Place a steamer basket in the pot.
4. Seal pot with lid and cook on high for 15 minutes.
5. Once done, allow to release pressure naturally for 5 minutes then release remaining using quick release. Remove lid.
6. Serve and enjoy.

Nutritional Value (Amount per Serving):

- Calories 40
- Fat 0.3 g
- Carbohydrates 8.7 g
- Sugar 2.1 g
- Protein 2.3 g
- Cholesterol 0 mg

Rosemary Garlic Zucchini

Preparation Time: 10 minutes

Cooking Time: 3 minutes

Serve: 2

Ingredients:

- 2 zucchini, cut into lengthwise
- 3 tbsp parmesan cheese, grated
- 1/2 cup water
- 1/2 tsp dried basil
- 1/4 tsp dried rosemary
- 2 tbsp olive oil
- 1/4 tsp garlic powder
- Pepper
- Salt

Directions:

1. Pout water into the instant pot.
2. Toss zucchini with oil, basil, rosemary, garlic, pepper, and salt.
3. Transfer zucchini into the steamer basket and place basket in the pot.
4. Seal pot with lid and cook on high for 3 minutes.
5. Once done, release pressure using quick release. Remove lid.
6. Transfer zucchini on a plate.
7. Top with cheese and serve.

Nutritional Value (Amount per Serving):

- Calories 177
- Fat 16 g
- Carbohydrates 7.2 g
- Sugar 3.5 g
- Protein 4.9 g
- Cholesterol 5 mg

Spicy Cauliflower

Preparation Time: 10 minutes

Cooking Time: 6 minutes

Serve: 2

Ingredients:

- 1/2 small cauliflower head, cut into florets
- 1 tbsp fresh parsley, chopped
- 1/2 cup water
- 1/4 tsp paprika
- 1/4 tsp turmeric
- 1/2 tsp ground cumin
- 1 tbsp olive oil
- 1/4 tsp chili powder
- 1/4 small onion, chopped
- 1 tomato, chopped
- Pepper
- Salt

Directions:

1. Add tomato, onion, and chili powder into the blender and blend until smooth.
2. Add oil into the inner pot of instant pot and set the pot on sauté mode.
3. Add blended tomato mixture into the pot and cook for 2-3 minutes.
4. Add paprika, cumin, turmeric, and pepper and stir for a minute.
5. Add remaining ingredients and stir well.
6. Seal pot with lid and cook on high for 3 minutes.
7. Once done, release pressure using quick release. Remove lid.
8. Stir and serve.

Nutritional Value (Amount per Serving):

- Calories 97
- Fat 7.5 g
- Carbohydrates 7.6 g
- Sugar 3.7 g
- Protein 2.2 g
- Cholesterol 0 mg

Chapter 6: Appetizers

Flavorful Italian Peppers

Preparation Time: 10 minutes

Cooking Time: 3 minutes

Serve: 4

Ingredients:

- 4 red bell peppers, cut into strips and remove seeds
- 1/2 tsp Italian seasoning
- 1/2 tsp garlic powder
- 1 tbsp vinegar
- 3 tbsp olive oil
- 1 cup of water
- Pepper
- Salt

Directions:

1. Add bell peppers and water into the instant pot.
2. Seal pot with lid and cook on high for 3 minutes.
3. Once done, release pressure using quick release. Remove lid.
4. In a small bowl, mix together oil, vinegar, garlic powder, Italian seasoning, pepper, and salt.
5. Once bell peppers are cooked then pour oil mixture over bell peppers and mix well.
6. Serve warm and enjoy.

Nutritional Value (Amount per Serving):

- Calories 132
- Fat 11 g
- Carbohydrates 9.4 g
- Sugar 6.2 g
- Protein 1.3 g
- Cholesterol 0 mg

Balsamic Bell Pepper Salsa

Preparation Time: 10 minutes

Cooking Time: 6 minutes

Serve: 2

Ingredients:

- 2 red bell peppers, chopped and seeds removed
- 1 cup grape tomatoes, halved
- 1/2 tbsp cayenne
- 1 tbsp balsamic vinegar
- 2 cup vegetable broth
- 1/2 cup sour cream
- 1/2 tsp garlic powder
- 1/2 onion, chopped
- Salt

Directions:

1. Add all ingredients except cream into the instant pot and stir well.
2. Seal pot with lid and cook on high for 6 minutes.
3. Once done, release pressure using quick release. Remove lid.
4. Add sour cream and stir well.
5. Blend the salsa mixture using an immersion blender until smooth.
6. Serve and enjoy.

Nutritional Value (Amount per Serving):

- Calories 235
- Fat 14.2 g
- Carbohydrates 19.8 g
- Sugar 10.7 g
- Protein 9.2 g
- Cholesterol 25 mg

Creamy Artichoke Dip

Preparation Time: 10 minutes

Cooking Time: 5 minutes

Serve: 8

Ingredients:

- 28 oz can artichoke hearts, drain and quartered
- 1 1/2 cups parmesan cheese, shredded
- 1 cup sour cream
- 1 cup mayonnaise
- 3.5 oz can green chilies
- 1 cup of water
- Pepper
- Salt

Directions:

1. Add artichokes, water, and green chilis into the instant pot.
2. Seal pot with the lid and select manual and set timer for 1 minute.
3. Once done, release pressure using quick release. Remove lid. Drain excess water.
4. Set instant pot on sauté mode. Add remaining ingredients and stir well and cook until cheese is melted.
5. Serve and enjoy.

Nutritional Value (Amount per Serving):

- Calories 262
- Fat 7.6 g
- Carbohydrates 14.4 g
- Sugar 2.8 g
- Protein 8.4 g
- Cholesterol 32 mg

Spicy Jalapeno Spinach Artichoke Dip

Preparation Time: 10 minutes

Cooking Time: 3 minutes

Serve: 15

Ingredients:

- 10 oz spinach, chopped
- 1/2 cup parmesan cheese, grated
- 8 oz Italian cheese, shredded
- 1/4 cup fresh parsley, chopped
- 2 tbsp jalapeno, diced
- 1 1/2 tbsp garlic, minced
- 2 tbsp green onion, chopped
- 14 oz cream cheese, cubed
- 18 oz jar marinated artichoke hearts, chopped
- 1 1/2 tbsp fresh lemon juice
- 1/2 cup vegetable stock

Directions:

1. Add all ingredients except parmesan cheese and Italian cheese into the instant pot and stir well.
2. Seal pot with lid and cook on high for 3 minutes.
3. Once done, allow to release pressure naturally for 5 minutes then release remaining using quick release. Remove lid.
4. Set pot on sauté mode. Add parmesan cheese and Italian cheese and stir well and cook until cheese is melted.
5. Serve and enjoy.

Nutritional Value (Amount per Serving):

- Calories 195
- Fat 16.3 g
- Carbohydrates 3.7 g
- Sugar 0.6 g
- Protein 6.7 g
- Cholesterol 42 mg

Healthy Spinach Dip

Preparation Time: 10 minutes

Cooking Time: 8 minutes

Serve: 4

Ingredients:

- 14 oz spinach
- 2 tbsp fresh lime juice
- 1 tbsp garlic, minced
- 2 tbsp olive oil
- 2 tbsp coconut cream
- Pepper
- Salt

Directions:

1. Add all ingredients except coconut cream into the instant pot and stir well.
2. Seal pot with lid and cook on low pressure for 8 minutes.
3. Once done, allow to release pressure naturally for 5 minutes then release remaining using quick release. Remove lid.
4. Add coconut cream and stir well and blend spinach mixture using a blender until smooth.
5. Serve and enjoy.

Nutritional Value (Amount per Serving):

- Calories 109
- Fat 9.2 g
- Carbohydrates 6.6 g
- Sugar 1.1 g
- Protein 3.2 g
- Cholesterol 0 mg

Olive Eggplant Spread

Preparation Time: 10 minutes

Cooking Time: 8 minutes

Serve: 12

Ingredients:

- 1 3/4 lbs eggplant, chopped
- 1/2 tbsp dried oregano
- 1/4 cup olives, pitted and chopped
- 1 tbsp tahini
- 1/4 cup fresh lime juice
- 1/2 cup water
- 2 garlic cloves
- 1/4 cup olive oil
- Salt

Directions:

1. Add oil into the inner pot of instant pot and set the pot on sauté mode.
2. Add eggplant and cook for 3-5 minutes. Turn off sauté mode.
3. Add water and salt and stir well.
4. Seal pot with lid and cook on high for 3 minutes.
5. Once done, release pressure using quick release. Remove lid.
6. Drain eggplant well and transfer into the food processor.
7. Add remaining ingredients into the food processor and process until smooth.
8. Serve and enjoy.

Nutritional Value (Amount per Serving):

- Calories 65
- Fat 5.3 g
- Carbohydrates 4.7 g
- Sugar 2 g
- Protein 0.9 g
- Cholesterol 0 mg

Spicy Pepper Eggplant Spread

Preparation Time: 10 minutes

Cooking Time: 9 minutes

Serve: 4

Ingredients:

- 3 cups Italian eggplants, cut into 1/-inch chunks
- 1/2 cup tomatoes, diced
- 1 cup red pepper, diced
- 1/2 tsp red pepper flakes
- 1 tbsp vinegar
- 2 tbsp garlic, minced
- 1/2 cup onion, diced
- 2 tbsp olive oil
- 1/4 cup water
- 1 tsp kosher salt

Directions:

1. Add oil into the inner pot of instant pot and set the pot on sauté mode.
2. Add red pepper and eggplant and sauté for 5 minutes.
3. Add remaining ingredients and stir everything well.
4. Seal pot with lid and cook on high for 4 minutes.
5. Once done, release pressure using quick release. Remove lid.
6. Mash the spread mixture using the spatula and serve.

Nutritional Value (Amount per Serving):

- Calories 237
- Fat 19.2 g
- Carbohydrates 18 g
- Sugar 2.8 g
- Protein 1 g
- Cholesterol 0 mg

Pepper Tomato Eggplant Spread

Preparation Time: 10 minutes

Cooking Time: 10 minutes

Serve: 3

Ingredients:

- 2 cups eggplant, chopped
- 1/4 cup vegetable broth
- 2 tbsp tomato paste
- 1/4 cup sun-dried tomatoes, minced
- 1 cup bell pepper, chopped
- 1 tsp garlic, minced
- 1 cup onion, chopped
- 3 tbsp olive oil
- Salt

Directions:

1. Add oil into the inner pot of instant pot and set the pot on sauté mode.
2. Add onion and sauté for 3 minutes.
3. Add eggplant, bell pepper, and garlic and sauté for 2 minutes.
4. Add remaining ingredients and stir well.
5. Seal pot with lid and cook on high for 5 minutes.
6. Once done, release pressure using quick release. Remove lid.
7. Lightly mash the eggplant mixture using a potato masher.
8. Stir well and serve.

Nutritional Value (Amount per Serving):

- Calories 178
- Fat 14.4 g
- Carbohydrates 12.8 g
- Sugar 7 g
- Protein 2.4 g
- Cholesterol 0 mg

Kidney Bean Spread

Preparation Time: 10 minutes

Cooking Time: 18 minutes

Serve: 4

Ingredients:

- 1 lb dry kidney beans, soaked overnight and drained
- 1 tsp garlic, minced
- 2 tbsp olive oil
- 1 tbsp fresh lemon juice
- 1 tbsp paprika
- 4 cups vegetable stock
- 1/2 cup onion, chopped
- Pepper
- Salt

Directions:

1. Add beans and stock into the instant pot.
2. Seal pot with lid and cook on high for 18 minutes.
3. Once done, allow to release pressure naturally. Remove lid.
4. Drain beans well and reserve 1/2 cup stock.
5. Transfer beans, reserve stock, and remaining ingredients into the food processor and process until smooth.
6. Serve and enjoy.

Nutritional Value (Amount per Serving):

- Calories 461
- Fat 8.6 g
- Carbohydrates 73 g
- Sugar 4 g
- Protein 26.4 g
- Cholesterol 0 mg

Spicy Chicken Dip

Preparation Time: 10 minutes

Cooking Time: 15 minutes

Serve: 10

Ingredients:

- 1 lb chicken breast, skinless and boneless
- 1/2 cup sour cream
- 8 oz cheddar cheese, shredded
- 1/2 cup chicken stock
- 2 jalapeno pepper, sliced
- 8 oz cream cheese
- Pepper
- Salt

Directions:

1. Add chicken, stock, jalapenos, and cream cheese into the instant pot.
2. Seal pot with lid and cook on high for 12 minutes.
3. Once done, release pressure using quick release. Remove lid.
4. Shred chicken using a fork.
5. Set pot on sauté mode. Add remaining ingredients and stir well and cook until cheese is melted.
6. Serve and enjoy.

Nutritional Value (Amount per Serving):

- Calories 248
- Fat 19 g
- Carbohydrates 1.6 g
- Sugar 0.3 g
- Protein 17.4 g
- Cholesterol 83 mg

Chapter 7: Poultry

Quinoa Chicken Bowls

Preparation Time: 10 minutes

Cooking Time: 6 minutes

Serve: 4

Ingredients:

- 1 lb chicken breasts, skinless, boneless, and cut into chunks
- 14 oz can chickpeas, drained and rinsed
- 1 cup olives, pitted and sliced
- 1 cup cherry tomatoes, halved
- 1 cucumber, sliced
- 2 tsp Greek seasoning
- 1 1/2 cups chicken broth
- 1 cup quinoa, rinsed and drained
- Pepper
- Salt

Directions:

1. Add broth and quinoa into the instant pot and stir well.
2. Season chicken with greek seasoning, pepper, and salt and place into the instant pot.
3. Seal pot with lid and cook on high for 6 minutes.
4. Once done, release pressure using quick release. Remove lid.
5. Stir quinoa and chicken mixture well.
6. Add remaining ingredients and stir everything well.
7. Serve immediately and enjoy it.

Nutritional Value (Amount per Serving):

- Calories 566
- Fat 16.4 g
- Carbohydrates 57.4 g
- Sugar 2.7 g
- Protein 46.8 g
- Cholesterol 101 mg

Garlic Thyme Chicken Drumsticks

Preparation Time: 10 minutes

Cooking Time: 18 minutes

Serve: 4

Ingredients:

- 8 chicken drumsticks, skin-on
- 2 tbsp balsamic vinegar
- 2/3 cup can tomatoes, diced
- 6 garlic cloves
- 1 tsp lemon zest, grated
- 1 tsp dried thyme
- 1/4 tsp red pepper flakes
- 1 1/2 onions, cut into wedges
- 1 tbsp olive oil
- Pepper
- Salt

Directions:

1. Add oil into the inner pot of instant pot and set the pot on sauté mode.
2. Add onion and 1/2 tsp salt and sauté for 2-3 minutes.
3. Add chicken, garlic, lemon zest, red pepper flakes, and thyme and mix well.
4. Add vinegar and tomatoes and stir well.
5. Seal pot with lid and cook on high for 15 minutes.
6. Once done, release pressure using quick release. Remove lid.
7. Stir well and serve.

Nutritional Value (Amount per Serving):

- Calories 220
- Fat 8.9 g
- Carbohydrates 7.8 g
- Sugar 3.2 g
- Protein 26.4 g
- Cholesterol 81 mg

Artichoke Olive Chicken

Preparation Time: 10 minutes

Cooking Time: 8 minutes

Serve: 6

Ingredients:

- 2 1/2 lbs chicken breasts, skinless and boneless
- 14 oz can artichokes
- 1/2 cup olives, pitted
- 3/4 cup prunes
- 1 tbsp capers
- 1 1/2 tbsp garlic, chopped
- 3 tbsp red wine vinegar
- 2 tsp dried oregano
- 1/3 cup wine
- Pepper
- Salt

Directions:

1. Add all ingredients except chicken into the instant pot and stir well.
2. Add chicken and mix well. Seal pot with lid and cook on high for 8 minutes.
3. Once done, allow to release pressure naturally for 10 minutes then release remaining using quick release. Remove lid.
4. Serve and enjoy.

Nutritional Value (Amount per Serving):

- Calories 472
- Fat 15.5 g
- Carbohydrates 22.7 g
- Sugar 8.9 g
- Protein 57.6 g
- Cholesterol 168 mg

Pesto Vegetable Chicken

Preparation Time: 10 minutes

Cooking Time: 25 minutes

Serve: 4

Ingredients:

- 1 1/2 lbs chicken thighs, skinless, boneless, and cut into pieces
- 1/2 cup chicken broth
- 1/4 cup fresh parsley, chopped
- 2 cups cherry tomatoes, halved
- 1 cup basil pesto
- 3/4 lb asparagus, trimmed and cut in half
- 2/3 cup sun-dried tomatoes, drained and chopped
- 2 tbsp olive oil
- Pepper
- Salt

Directions:

1. Add oil into the inner pot of instant pot and set the pot on sauté mode.
2. Add chicken and sauté for 5 minutes.
3. Add remaining ingredients except for tomatoes and stir well.
4. Seal pot with a lid and select manual and set timer for 15 minutes.
5. Once done, release pressure using quick release. Remove lid.
6. Add tomatoes and stir well. Again seal the pot and select manual and set timer for 5 minutes.
7. Release pressure using quick release. Remove lid.
8. Stir well and serve.

Nutritional Value (Amount per Serving):

- Calories 459
- Fat 20.5 g
- Carbohydrates 14.9 g
- Sugar 9.2 g
- Protein 9.2 g
- Cholesterol 151 mg

Flavorful Mediterranean Chicken

Preparation Time: 10 minutes

Cooking Time: 20 minutes

Serve: 8

Ingredients:

- 2 lbs chicken thighs
- 1/2 cup olives
- 28 oz can tomato, diced
- 1 1/2 tsp dried oregano
- 2 tsp dried parsley
- 1/2 tsp ground coriander powder
- 1/4 tsp chili pepper
- 1 tsp onion powder
- 1 sp paprika
- 2 cups onion, chopped
- 2 tbsp olive oil
- Pepper
- Salt

Directions:

1. Add oil into the inner pot of instant pot and set the pot on sauté mode.
2. Add chicken and cook until browned. Transfer chicken on a plate.
3. Add onion and sauté for 5 minutes.
4. Add all spices, tomatoes, and salt and cook for 2-3 minutes.
5. Return chicken to the pot and stir everything well.
6. Seal pot with lid and cook on high for 8 minutes.
7. Once done, release pressure using quick release. Remove lid.
8. Add olives and stir well.
9. Serve and enjoy.

Nutritional Value (Amount per Serving):

- Calories 292
- Fat 13 g
- Carbohydrates 8.9 g
- Sugar 4.8 g
- Protein 34.3 g
- Cholesterol 101 mg

Tasty Turkey Chili

Preparation Time: 10 minutes

Cooking Time: 25 minutes

Serve: 4

Ingredients:

- 1 lb cooked turkey, shredded
- 2 cups chicken broth
- 1 tsp tomato paste
- 1 small onion, chopped
- 1 tbsp Italian seasoning
- 1 tsp garlic powder
- 1 tbsp cumin, roasted
- 1 tbsp chili powder
- 2 cups tomatoes, crushed
- 1 tsp garlic, minced
- 14 oz can red beans, drained
- 14 oz can chickpeas, drained
- 1/2 cup corn
- 2 carrots, peeled and chopped
- 1/2 cup celery, chopped
- 1/4 cup edamame
- 2 tbsp olive oil
- Pepper
- Salt

Directions:

1. Add all ingredients into the instant pot and stir everything well.
2. Seal pot with lid and cook on high for 15 minutes.
3. Once done, allow to release pressure naturally. Remove lid.
4. Set pot on sauté mode and cook for 5-10 minutes or until chili thicken.
5. Stir well and serve.

Nutritional Value (Amount per Serving):

- Calories 593
- Fat 18.1 g
- Carbohydrates 56 g
- Sugar 7.3 g
- Protein 50.9 g
- Cholesterol 88 mg

Flavorful Chicken Tacos

Preparation Time: 10 minutes

Cooking Time: 10 minutes

Serve: 3

Ingredients:

- 2 chicken breasts, skinless and boneless
- 1 tbsp chili powder
- 1/2 tsp ground cumin
- 1/2 tsp garlic powder
- 1/4 tsp onion powder
- 1/2 tsp paprika
- 4 oz can green chilis, diced
- 1/4 cup chicken broth
- 14 oz can tomatoes, diced
- Pepper
- Salt

Directions:

1. Add all ingredients except chicken into the instant pot and stir well.
2. Add chicken and stir. Seal pot with lid and cook on high for 10 minutes.
3. Once done, allow to release pressure naturally for 5 minutes then release remaining using quick release. Remove lid.
4. Remove chicken from pot and shred using a fork.
5. Return shredded chicken to the pot and stir well.
6. Serve and enjoy.

Nutritional Value (Amount per Serving):

- Calories 237
- Fat 8 g
- Carbohydrates 10.8 g
- Sugar 5 g
- Protein 30.5 g
- Cholesterol 87 mg

Quick Chicken with Mushrooms

Preparation Time: 10 minutes

Cooking Time: 22 minutes

Serve: 6

Ingredients:

- 2 lbs chicken breasts, skinless and boneless
- 1/2 cup heavy cream
- 1/3 cup water
- 3/4 lb mushrooms, sliced
- 3 tbsp olive oil
- 1 tsp Italian seasoning
- Pepper
- Salt

Directions:

1. Add oil into the inner pot of instant pot and set the pot on sauté mode.
2. Season chicken with Italian seasoning, pepper, and salt.
3. Add chicken to the pot and sauté for 5 minutes. Remove chicken from pot and set aside.
4. Add mushrooms and sauté for 5 minutes or until mushrooms are lightly brown.
5. Return chicken to the pot. Add water and stir well.
6. Seal pot with a lid and select manual and set timer for 12 minutes.
7. Once done, release pressure using quick release. Remove lid.
8. Remove chicken from pot and place on a plate.
9. Set pot on sauté mode. Add heavy cream and stir well and cook for 5 minutes.
10. Pour mushroom sauce over chicken and serve.

Nutritional Value (Amount per Serving):

- Calories 396
- Fat 22.3 g
- Carbohydrates 2.2 g
- Sugar 1.1 g
- Protein 45.7 g
- Cholesterol 149 mg

Moroccan Spiced Chicken

Preparation Time: 10 minutes

Cooking Time: 20 minutes

Serve: 4

Ingredients:

- 1 lb chicken thighs, boneless and cut into chunks
- 1 cup can tomato, crushed
- 1/2 tsp red pepper flakes
- 1 tsp dried parsley
- 1/2 tsp coriander
- 1 tsp cumin
- 14 oz can chickpeas, drained and rinsed
- 2 tomatoes, chopped
- 1 tbsp garlic, minced
- 1 onion, sliced
- 2 red peppers, diced
- 1 tbsp olive oil
- Pepper
- Salt

Directions:

1. Add oil into the inner pot of instant pot and set the pot on sauté mode.
2. Add onion and garlic and sauté for 5 minutes.
3. Add chicken and cook for 5 minutes.
4. Add remaining ingredients and stir well.
5. Seal pot with lid and cook on high for 10 minutes.
6. Once done, release pressure using quick release. Remove lid.
7. Stir well and serve.

Nutritional Value (Amount per Serving):

- Calories 416
- Fat 21.3 g
- Carbohydrates 32.3 g
- Sugar 4 g
- Protein 26.1 g
- Cholesterol 96 mg

Delicious Gyro Chicken

Preparation Time: 10 minutes

Cooking Time: 12 minutes

Serve: 3

Ingredients:

- 1 lb chicken thighs
- 1 cup chicken broth
- 1 tsp garlic, minced
- 1 tbsp fresh lemon juice
- 1 tbsp olive oil
- 2 tbsp fresh cilantro, chopped
- 1 tbsp green onion, chopped
- 1/2 tsp oregano
- 1/2 tsp cumin powder
- 1/2 tsp ground cinnamon
- 1/2 tsp paprika
- 1/2 tsp Adobo seasoning
- 1 onion, sliced
- Pepper
- Salt

Directions:

1. Season chicken with oregano, cinnamon, cumin, paprika, adobo seasoning, pepper, and salt and place into the instant pot.
2. Pour remaining ingredients over chicken.
3. Seal pot with lid and cook on high for 12 minutes.
4. Once done, release pressure using quick release. Remove lid.
5. Stir well and serve.

Nutritional Value (Amount per Serving):

- Calories 362
- Fat 16.6 g
- Carbohydrates 5.2 g
- Sugar 2 g
- Protein 46.1 g
- Cholesterol 135 mg

Chapter 8: Beef

Flavorful Beef Bourguignon

Preparation Time: 10 minutes

Cooking Time: 20 minutes

Serve: 4

Ingredients:

- 1 1/2 lbs beef chuck roast, cut into chunks
- 2/3 cup beef stock
- 2 tbsp fresh thyme
- 1 bay leaf
- 1 tsp garlic, minced
- 8 oz mushrooms, sliced
- 2 tbsp tomato paste
- 2/3 cup dry red wine
- 1 onion, sliced
- 4 carrots, cut into chunks
- 1 tbsp olive oil
- Pepper
- Salt

Directions:

1. Add oil into the instant pot and set the pot on sauté mode.
2. Add meat and sauté until brown. Add onion and sauté until softened.
3. Add remaining ingredients and stir well.
4. Seal pot with lid and cook on high for 12 minutes.
5. Once done, allow to release pressure naturally. Remove lid.
6. Stir well and serve.

Nutritional Value (Amount per Serving):

- Calories 744
- Fat 51.3 g
- Carbohydrates 14.5 g
- Sugar 6.5 g
- Protein 48.1 g
- Cholesterol 175 mg

Delicious Beef Chili

Preparation Time: 10 minutes

Cooking Time: 35 minutes

Serve: 8

Ingredients:

- 2 lbs ground beef
- 1 tsp olive oil
- 1 tsp garlic, minced
- 1 small onion, chopped
- 2 tbsp chili powder
- 1 tsp oregano
- 1/2 tsp thyme
- 28 oz can tomatoes, crushed
- 2 cups beef stock
- 2 carrots, chopped
- 3 sweet potatoes, peeled and cubed
- Pepper
- Salt

Directions:

1. Add oil into the instant pot and set the pot on sauté mode.
2. Add meat and cook until brown.
3. Add remaining ingredients and stir well.
4. Seal pot with lid and cook on high for 35 minutes.
5. Once done, allow to release pressure naturally. Remove lid.
6. Stir well and serve.

Nutritional Value (Amount per Serving):

- Calories 302
- Fat 8.2 g
- Carbohydrates 19.2 g
- Sugar 4.8 g
- Protein 37.1 g
- Cholesterol 101 mg

Greek Chuck Roast

Preparation Time: 10 minutes

Cooking Time: 35 minutes

Serve: 6

Ingredients:

- 3 lbs beef chuck roast, boneless and cut into chunks
- 1/2 tsp dried basil
- 1 tsp oregano, chopped
- 1 small onion, chopped
- 1 cup tomatoes, diced
- 2 cups chicken broth
- 1 tbsp olive oil
- 1 tbsp garlic, minced
- Pepper
- Salt

Directions:

1. Add oil into the instant pot and set the pot on sauté mode.
2. Add onion and garlic and sauté for 3-5 minutes.
3. Add meat and sauté for 5 minutes.
4. Add remaining ingredients and stir well.
5. Seal pot with lid and cook on high for 25 minutes.
6. Once done, allow to release pressure naturally. Remove lid.
7. Serve and enjoy.

Nutritional Value (Amount per Serving):

- Calories 869
- Fat 66 g
- Carbohydrates 3.2 g
- Sugar 1.5 g
- Protein 61.5 g
- Cholesterol 234 mg

Beef with Tomatoes

Preparation Time: 10 minutes

Cooking Time: 40 minutes

Serve: 4

Ingredients:

- 2 lb beef roast, sliced
- 1 tbsp chives, chopped
- 1 tsp garlic, minced
- 1/2 tsp chili powder
- 2 tbsp olive oil
- 1 onion, chopped
- 1 cup beef stock
- 1 tbsp oregano, chopped
- 1 cup tomatoes, chopped
- Pepper
- Salt

Directions:

1. Add oil into the instant pot and set the pot on sauté mode.
2. Add garlic, onion, and chili powder and sauté for 5 minutes.
3. Add meat and cook for 5 minutes.
4. Add remaining ingredients and stir well.
5. Seal pot with lid and cook on high for 30 minutes.
6. Once done, allow to release pressure naturally for 10 minutes then release remaining using quick release. Remove lid.
7. Stir well and serve.

Nutritional Value (Amount per Serving):

- Calories 511
- Fat 21.6 g
- Carbohydrates 5.6 g
- Sugar 2.5 g
- Protein 70.4 g
- Cholesterol 203 mg

Rosemary Beef Eggplant

Preparation Time: 10 minutes

Cooking Time: 30 minutes

Serve: 4

Ingredients:

- 1 lb beef stew meat, cubed
- 2 tbsp green onion, chopped
- 1/4 tsp red pepper flakes
- 1/2 tsp dried rosemary
- 1/2 tsp paprika
- 1 cup chicken stock
- 1 onion, chopped
- 1 eggplant, cubed
- 2 tbsp olive oil
- Pepper
- Salt

Directions:

1. Add oil into the instant pot and set the pot on sauté mode.
2. Add meat and onion and sauté for 5 minutes.
3. Add remaining ingredients and stir well.
4. Seal pot with lid and cook on high for 25 minutes.
5. Once done, allow to release pressure naturally. Remove lid.
6. Serve and enjoy.

Nutritional Value (Amount per Serving):

- Calories 315
- Fat 14.5 g
- Carbohydrates 10 g
- Sugar 4.9 g
- Protein 36.1 g
- Cholesterol 101 mg

Delicious Ground Beef

Preparation Time: 10 minutes

Cooking Time: 10 minutes

Serve: 4

Ingredients:

- 1 lb ground beef
- 1 tbsp olive oil
- 2 tbsp tomato paste
- 1 cup chicken broth
- 12 oz cheddar cheese, shredded
- 1 tbsp Italian seasoning
- Pepper
- Salt

Directions:

1. Add oil into the instant pot and set the pot on sauté mode.
2. Add meat and cook until browned.
3. Add remaining ingredients except for cheese and stir well.
4. Seal pot with lid and cook on high for 7 minutes.
5. Once done, release pressure using quick release. Remove lid.
6. Add cheese and stir well and cook on sauté mode until cheese is melted.
7. Serve and enjoy.

Nutritional Value (Amount per Serving):

- Calories 610
- Fat 40.2 g
- Carbohydrates 3.2 g
- Sugar 1.9 g
- Protein 57.2 g
- Cholesterol 193 mg

Beef Curry

Preparation Time: 10 minutes

Cooking Time: 30 minutes

Serve: 2

Ingredients:

- 1/2 lb beef stew meat, cubed
- 1 bell peppers, sliced
- 1 cup beef stock
- 1 tbsp fresh ginger, grated
- 1/2 tsp ground cumin
- 1 tsp ground coriander
- 1/2 tsp cayenne pepper
- 1/2 cup sun-roasted tomatoes, diced
- 2 tbsp olive oil
- 1 tsp garlic, crushed
- 1 green chili peppers, chopped

Directions:

1. Add all ingredients into the instant pot and stir well.
2. Seal pot with lid and cook on high for 30 minutes.
3. Once done, allow to release pressure naturally. Remove lid.
4. Serve and enjoy.

Nutritional Value (Amount per Serving):

- Calories 391
- Fat 21.9 g
- Carbohydrates 11.6 g
- Sugar 5.8 g
- Protein 37.4 g
- Cholesterol 101 mg

Artichoke Beef Roast

Preparation Time: 10 minutes

Cooking Time: 45 minutes

Serve: 6

Ingredients:

- 2 lbs beef roast, cubed
- 1 tbsp garlic, minced
- 1 onion, chopped
- 1/2 tsp paprika
- 1 tbsp parsley, chopped
- 2 tomatoes, chopped
- 1 tbsp capers, chopped
- 10 oz can artichokes, drained and chopped
- 2 cups chicken stock
- 1 tbsp olive oil
- Pepper
- Salt

Directions:

1. Add oil into the instant pot and set the pot on sauté mode.
2. Add garlic and onion and sauté for 5 minutes.
3. Add meat and cook until brown.
4. Add remaining ingredients and stir well.
5. Seal pot with lid and cook on high for 35 minutes.
6. Once done, allow to release pressure naturally. Remove lid.
7. Serve and enjoy.

Nutritional Value (Amount per Serving):

- Calories 344
- Fat 12.2 g
- Carbohydrates 9.2 g
- Sugar 2.6 g
- Protein 48.4 g
- Cholesterol 135 mg

Moist Shredded Beef

Preparation Time: 10 minutes
Cooking Time: 20 minutes
Serve: 8

Ingredients:

- 2 lbs beef chuck roast, cut into chunks
- 1/2 tbsp dried red pepper
- 1 tbsp Italian seasoning
- 1 tbsp garlic, minced
- 2 tbsp vinegar
- 14 oz can fire-roasted tomatoes
- 1/2 cup bell pepper, chopped
- 1/2 cup carrots, chopped
- 1 cup onion, chopped
- 1 tsp salt

Directions:

1. Add all ingredients into the inner pot of instant pot and set the pot on sauté mode.
2. Seal pot with lid and cook on high for 20 minutes.
3. Once done, release pressure using quick release. Remove lid.
4. Shred the meat using a fork.
5. Stir well and serve.

Nutritional Value (Amount per Serving):

- Calories 456
- Fat 32.7 g
- Carbohydrates 7.7 g
- Sugar 4.1 g
- Protein 31 g
- Cholesterol 118 mg

Beef Shawarma

Preparation Time: 10 minutes

Cooking Time: 10 minutes

Serve: 2

Ingredients:

- 1/2 lb ground beef
- 1/4 tsp cinnamon
- 1/2 tsp dried oregano
- 1 cup cabbage, cut into strips
- 1/2 cup bell pepper, sliced
- 1/4 tsp ground coriander
- 1/4 tsp cumin
- 1/4 tsp cayenne pepper
- 1/4 tsp ground allspice
- 1/2 cup onion, chopped
- 1/2 tsp salt

Directions:

1. Set instant pot on sauté mode.
2. Add meat to the pot and sauté until brown.
3. Add remaining ingredients and stir well.
4. Seal pot with lid and cook on high for 5 minutes.
5. Once done, release pressure using quick release. Remove lid.
6. Stir and serve.

Nutritional Value (Amount per Serving):

- Calories 245
- Fat 7.4 g
- Carbohydrates 7.9 g
- Sugar 3.9 g
- Protein 35.6 g
- Cholesterol 101 mg

Chapter 9: Pork

Pork with Carrots Potatoes

Preparation Time: 10 minutes

Cooking Time: 15 minutes

Serve: 2

Ingredients:

- 2 pork chops, boneless
- 1/4 cup balsamic vinegar
- 2 tbsp honey
- 1 1/2 tsp ground ginger
- 1 tsp curry powder
- 1/2 cup chicken stock
- 1 tbsp olive oil
- 3 carrots, chopped
- 3 small potatoes, cubed
- 2 garlic cloves, chopped
- Pepper
- Salt

Directions:

1. Add oil into the instant pot and set the pot on sauté mode.
2. Add pork chops into the pot and brown them from both the sides.
3. Add remaining ingredients to the pot and stir well.
4. Seal pot with lid and cook on high for 10 minutes.
5. Once done, allow to release pressure naturally. Open the lid.
6. Serve and enjoy.

Nutritional Value (Amount per Serving):

- Calories 615
- Fat 27.5 g
- Carbohydrates 69.4 g
- Sugar 25.1 g
- Protein 23.7 g
- Cholesterol 69 mg

Pork Roast with Potatoes

Preparation Time: 10 minutes

Cooking Time: 30 minutes

Serve: 4

Ingredients:

- 2 lbs pork roast, sliced
- 1 tbsp fresh parsley, chopped
- 1 cup chicken stock
- 1 tbsp olive oil
- 1/2 tsp rosemary, chopped
- 1 tsp chili powder
- 1 cup heavy cream
- 1 onion, chopped
- 2 sweet potatoes, peeled and cubed
- Pepper
- Salt

Directions:

1. Add oil into the inner pot of instant pot and set the pot on sauté mode.
2. Add onion and meat and sauté for 5 minutes.
3. Add remaining ingredients except for heavy cream and stir well.
4. Seal pot with lid and cook on high for 25 minutes.
5. Once done, allow to release pressure naturally for 10 minutes then release remaining using quick release. Remove lid.
6. Stir in heavy cream and serve.

Nutritional Value (Amount per Serving):

- Calories 664
- Fat 36.4 g
- Carbohydrates 14.6 g
- Sugar 1.6 g
- Protein 66.4 g
- Cholesterol 236 mg

Garlic Parsley Pork Chops

Preparation Time: 10 minutes
Cooking Time: 25 minutes
Serve: 4

Ingredients:

- 4 pork chops, boneless
- 1 tbsp garlic, minced
- 1/2 cup tomato puree
- 1 cup chicken stock
- 1 onion, chopped
- 1 tbsp fresh parsley, chopped
- 1 tbsp olive oil
- Pepper
- Salt

Directions:

1. Add oil into the inner pot of instant pot and set the pot on sauté mode.
2. Add garlic and onion and sauté for 2 minutes.
3. Add pork chops and sauté for 3 minutes.
4. Add remaining ingredients and stir well.
5. Seal pot with lid and cook on high for 20 minutes.
6. Once done, allow to release pressure naturally for 10 minutes then release remaining using quick release. Remove lid.
7. Stir and serve.

Nutritional Value (Amount per Serving):

- Calories 315
- Fat 23.6 g
- Carbohydrates 6.3 g
- Sugar 2.9 g
- Protein 19.1 g
- Cholesterol 69 mg

Pork with Vegetables

Preparation Time: 10 minutes

Cooking Time: 22 minutes

Serve: 4

Ingredients:

- 1 lb pork, cut into chunks
- 2 potatoes, quarters
- 1 lb green beans
- 3 tomatoes, chopped
- 2 celery sticks, sliced
- 2 carrots, sliced
- 1/2 cup olive oil
- 1 onion, chopped
- Pepper
- Salt

Directions:

1. Add oil into the inner pot of instant pot and set the pot on sauté mode.
2. Add meat and cook for 5 minutes.
3. Add remaining ingredients and stir everything well.
4. Seal pot with lid and cook on high for 17 minutes.
5. Once done, release pressure using quick release. Remove lid.
6. Stir well and serve.

Nutritional Value (Amount per Serving):

- Calories 527
- Fat 29.6 g
- Carbohydrates 34.1 g
- Sugar 7.9 g
- Protein 34.9 g
- Cholesterol 83 mg

Herb Pork

Preparation Time: 10 minutes

Cooking Time: 30 minutes

Serve: 4

Ingredients:

- 1 lb pork stew meat, cut into cubes
- 1 cup can tomato, crushed
- 1 tbsp olive oil
- 1/2 tsp dried oregano
- 1 tbsp tarragon, chopped
- 1 onion, chopped
- Pepper
- Salt

Directions:

1. Add oil into the inner pot of instant pot and set the pot on sauté mode.
2. Add onion and meat and sauté for 5 minutes.
3. Add remaining ingredients and stir well.
4. Seal pot with lid and cook on high for 25 minutes.
5. Once done, allow to release pressure naturally. Remove lid.
6. Serve and enjoy.

Nutritional Value (Amount per Serving):

- Calories 291
- Fat 14.6 g
- Carbohydrates 4.8 g
- Sugar 1.2 g
- Protein 34 g
- Cholesterol 98 mg

Pork Chops with Sprouts

Preparation Time: 10 minutes

Cooking Time: 30 minutes

Serve: 4

Ingredients:

- 4 pork chops
- 1 tbsp parsley, chopped
- 1 cup chicken stock
- 1 tbsp Italian seasoning
- 1 lb Brussels sprouts
- Pepper
- Salt

Directions:

1. Add all ingredients into the inner pot of instant pot and stir well.
2. Seal pot with lid and cook on high for 30 minutes.
3. Once done, allow to release pressure naturally. Remove lid.
4. Serve and enjoy.

Nutritional Value (Amount per Serving):

- Calories 319
- Fat 21.5 g
- Carbohydrates 11 g
- Sugar 3 g
- Protein 22.1 g
- Cholesterol 71 mg

Simple Lemon Pepper Pork Chops

Preparation Time: 10 minutes

Cooking Time: 15 minutes

Serve: 2

Ingredients:

- 1/2 lb pork chops
- 1 1/2 tbsp lemon pepper seasoning
- 1/4 cup chicken stock
- Salt

Directions:

1. Season pork chops with lemon pepper seasoning and salt.
2. Set pot on sauté mode.
3. Add pork chops and sauté until brown. Pour stock over pork chops.
4. Seal pot with lid and cook on high for 10 minutes.
5. Once done, release pressure using quick release. Remove lid.
6. Serve and enjoy.

Nutritional Value (Amount per Serving):

- Calories 376
- Fat 28.4 g
- Carbohydrates 3.2 g
- Sugar 0.1 g
- Protein 26.1 g
- Cholesterol 98 mg

Cheese Pork Chops

Preparation Time: 10 minutes

Cooking Time: 15 minutes

Serve: 2

Ingredients:

- 2 pork chops, boneless
- 1/2 tbsp olive oil
- 1/2 tbsp Italian seasoning
- 3 oz feta cheese, crumbled
- 3/4 cup chicken stock
- 1/2 tsp garlic powder
- Pepper
- Salt

Directions:

1. Season pork chops with Italian seasoning, garlic powder, pepper, and salt and set aside.
2. Add oil into the instant pot and set the pot on sauté mode.
3. Add pork chops and cook until brown. Pour stock over pork chops.
4. Seal pot with lid and cook on high for 10 minutes.
5. Once done, allow to release pressure naturally for 10 minutes then release remaining using quick release. Remove lid.
6. Top with cheese and serve.

Nutritional Value (Amount per Serving):

- Calories 415
- Fat 33.7 g
- Carbohydrates 2.9 g
- Sugar 2.5 g
- Protein 24.4 g
- Cholesterol 109 mg

Lime Salsa Pork Chops

Preparation Time: 10 minutes

Cooking Time: 25 minutes

Serve: 4

Ingredients:

- 1 1/2 lbs pork chops
- 1/2 tsp garlic powder
- 1/2 tsp ground cumin
- 2 tbsp lime juice
- 1/2 cup salsa
- 1 tbsp olive oil
- Pepper
- Salt

Directions:

1. Add oil into the inner pot of instant pot and set the pot on sauté mode.
2. Add pork chops and sauté until brown.
3. Add remaining ingredients and stir well.
4. Seal pot with lid and cook on high for 15 minutes.
5. Once done, release pressure using quick release. Remove lid.
6. Serve and enjoy.

Nutritional Value (Amount per Serving):

- Calories 591
- Fat 45.9 g
- Carbohydrates 4.3 g
- Sugar 1.5 g
- Protein 38.9 g
- Cholesterol 146 mg

Pork Rice

Preparation Time: 10 minutes

Cooking Time: 30 minutes

Serve: 2

Ingredients:

- 1 lb pork tenderloin, cut into 1-inch pieces
- 1/2 cup rice
- 7 oz can black beans, rinsed and drained
- 1 tsp garlic, chopped
- 1/4 cup orange juice
- 1 tbsp fresh cilantro, chopped
- 1/2 tbsp fresh lime juice
- 1 cup chicken broth
- 1 tbsp olive oil
- 1/2 tsp ground cumin
- Salt

Directions:

1. Add oil into the instant pot and set the pot on sauté mode.
2. Add meat to the pot and sauté for 5 minutes.
3. Stir in orange juice, cumin, garlic, broth, rice, and beans.
4. Seal pot with lid and cook on high for 12 minutes.
5. Once done, release pressure using quick release. Remove lid.
6. Stir in lime juice and garnish with cilantro.
7. Serve and enjoy.

Nutritional Value (Amount per Serving):

- Calories 685
- Fat 16.5 g
- Carbohydrates 59.8 g
- Sugar 4 g
- Protein 70.9 g
- Cholesterol 166 mg

Chapter 10: Lamb

Sweet Potato lamb

Preparation Time: 10 minutes

Cooking Time: 35 minutes

Serve: 4

Ingredients:

- 1 lb lamb shoulder, cut into chunks
- 2 tbsp olive oil
- 1 cup beef stock
- 2 sweet potatoes, cubed
- 1 tsp garlic, minced
- 1 onion, chopped
- 1 carrot, chopped
- Pepper
- Salt

Directions:

1. Add oil into the inner pot of instant pot and set the pot on sauté mode.
2. Add garlic and onion and sauté for 2 minutes.
3. Add meat and sauté for 3 minutes.
4. Add remaining ingredients and stir well.
5. Seal pot with lid and cook on high for 30 minutes.
6. Once done, allow to release pressure naturally. Remove lid.
7. Stir well and serve.

Nutritional Value (Amount per Serving):

- Calories 338
- Fat 15.5 g
- Carbohydrates 14.8 g
- Sugar 2.1 g
- Protein 33.6 g
- Cholesterol 102 mg

Italian Lamb Stew

Preparation Time: 10 minutes

Cooking Time: 30 minutes

Serve: 4

Ingredients:

- 2 lbs lamb, cut into chunks
- 1/2 cup cilantro, chopped
- 1 tsp dried oregano
- 1 tbsp olive oil
- 1 cup tomatoes, chopped
- 1 cup olives, pitted and sliced
- 1 onion, chopped
- 1 tbsp garlic, minced
- Pepper
- Salt

Directions:

1. Add oil into the inner pot of instant pot and set the pot on sauté mode.
2. Add oregano, garlic, and onion and sauté for 5 minutes.
3. Add meat and sauté for 5 minutes.
4. Add the rest of the ingredients and stir well.
5. Seal pot with lid and cook on high for 20 minutes.
6. Once done, allow to release pressure naturally. Remove lid.
7. Serve and enjoy.

Nutritional Value (Amount per Serving):

- Calories 514
- Fat 23.9 g
- Carbohydrates 7.4 g
- Sugar 2.4 g
- Protein 64.9 g
- Cholesterol 204 mg

Flavors Lamb Ribs

Preparation Time: 10 minutes

Cooking Time: 25 minutes

Serve: 4

Ingredients:

- 4 lamb ribs
- 2 tomatoes, chopped
- 2 tbsp olive oil
- 1 1/2 cups chicken stock
- 1 tbsp sage, chopped
- 1 tbsp garlic, minced
- Pepper
- Salt

Directions:

1. Add oil into the inner pot of instant pot and set the pot on sauté mode.
2. Add lamb ribs and sear for 5 minutes.
3. Add remaining ingredients except for heavy cream and stir well.
4. Seal pot with lid and cook on high for 20 minutes.
5. Once done, allow to release pressure naturally for 10 minutes then release remaining using quick release. Remove lid.
6. Serve and enjoy.

Nutritional Value (Amount per Serving):

- Calories 539
- Fat 46.1 g
- Carbohydrates 10.9 g
- Sugar 7.2 g
- Protein 22.6 g
- Cholesterol 0 mg

Lamb Shanks

Preparation Time: 10 minutes

Cooking Time: 25 minutes

Serve: 4

Ingredients:

- 4 lamb shanks
- 1 tomato, chopped
- 1/4 cup leeks, chopped
- 2 celery stalks, chopped
- 1 tsp garlic, minced
- 1 onion, chopped
- 1/4 cup balsamic vinegar
- 3 tbsp olive oil
- 3 cups beef broth
- 8 oz mushrooms, sliced
- 1 tsp dried rosemary
- Pepper
- Salt

Directions:

1. Add all ingredients into the inner pot of instant pot and stir well.
2. Seal pot with lid and cook on high for 25 minutes.
3. Once done, allow to release pressure naturally. Remove lid.
4. Stir well and serve.

Nutritional Value (Amount per Serving):

- Calories 763
- Fat 35.8 g
- Carbohydrates 7.3 g
- Sugar 3.5 g
- Protein 97.9 g
- Cholesterol 83 mg

Tomato Oregano Lamb Stew

Preparation Time: 10 minutes

Cooking Time: 40 minutes

Serve: 4

Ingredients:

- 4 lamb shanks
- 2 cups beef stock
- 1 tbsp oregano, chopped
- 1 1/2 cups tomatoes, chopped
- 1 tsp garlic, minced
- 1 onion, chopped
- 2 tbsp olive oil
- Pepper
- Salt

Directions:

1. Add oil into the inner pot of instant pot and set the pot on sauté mode.
2. Add lamb and sear for 5 minutes.
3. Add the rest of the ingredients and stir well.
4. Seal pot with lid and cook on low pressure for 35 minutes.
5. Once done, allow to release pressure naturally. Remove lid.
6. Serve and enjoy.

Nutritional Value (Amount per Serving):

- Calories 704
- Fat 31.5 g
- Carbohydrates 6.2 g
- Sugar 3 g
- Protein 94.2 g
- Cholesterol 294 mg

Lamb Stew

Preparation Time: 10 minutes

Cooking Time: 30 minutes

Serve: 4

Ingredients:

- 2 lbs lamb shoulder, cut into cubes
- 1 tsp dried basil
- 1 tsp dried oregano
- 1 tbsp olive oil
- 2 onion, chopped
- 14 oz can tomatoes, chopped
- 1 tbsp garlic, minced
- Pepper
- Salt

Directions:

1. Add oil into the inner pot of instant pot and set the pot on sauté mode.
2. Add meat, onion, and garlic and sauté for 5 minutes.
3. Add remaining ingredients and stir well.
4. Seal pot with lid and cook on high for 25 minutes.
5. Once done, allow to release pressure naturally for 10 minutes then release remaining using quick release. Remove lid.
6. Stir well and serve.

Nutritional Value (Amount per Serving):

- Calories 499
- Fat 20.2 g
- Carbohydrates 11.2 g
- Sugar 5.7 g
- Protein 65.4 g
- Cholesterol 204 mg

Italian Lamb Tomatoes

Preparation Time: 10 minutes

Cooking Time: 10 minutes

Serve: 4

Ingredients:

- 1 lb lamb loin, cut into chunks
- 1/4 tsp garlic powder
- 1 tsp cumin powder
- 1/2 tsp dried rosemary
- 1 tbsp olive oil
- 1 cup beef broth
- 1/2 cup fresh parsley, chopped
- 1 cup grape tomatoes
- 1 onion, chopped
- Pepper
- Salt

Directions:

1. Add oil into the inner pot of instant pot and set the pot on sauté mode.
2. Add lamb ribs and sear for 3 minutes.
3. Add remaining ingredients and stir well.
4. Seal pot with lid and cook on high for 7 minutes.
5. Once done, release pressure using quick release. Remove lid.
6. Serve and enjoy.

Nutritional Value (Amount per Serving):

- Calories 386
- Fat 30.3 g
- Carbohydrates 5.5 g
- Sugar 2.6 g
- Protein 21.3 g
- Cholesterol 80 mg

Healthy Lamb & Couscous

Preparation Time: 10 minutes

Cooking Time: 43 minutes

Serve: 4

Ingredients:

- 4 lamb chops
- 2 celery stalks, chopped
- 1 tbsp olive oil
- 1 tbsp basil, chopped
- 1 tbsp oregano, chopped
- 1 tbsp almonds, chopped
- 3 cups beef stock
- 1 1/2 cusp couscous
- Pepper
- Salt

Directions:

1. Add oil into the inner pot of instant pot and set the pot on sauté mode.
2. Add the meat into the pot and sauté for 3 minutes.
3. Add the rest of the ingredients and stir well.
4. Seal pot with lid and cook on low pressure for 40 minutes.
5. Once done, allow to release pressure naturally. Remove lid.
6. Serve and enjoy.

Nutritional Value (Amount per Serving):

- Calories 908
- Fat 29.2 g
- Carbohydrates 51.7 g
- Sugar 0.2 g
- Protein 102.7 g
- Cholesterol 294 mg

Lamb with Sprouts

Preparation Time: 10 minutes

Cooking Time: 15 minutes

Serve: 4

Ingredients:

- 1 lb lamb, cut into chunks
- 1 tsp rosemary
- 1/2 tsp dried sage
- 1/2 tsp chili powder
- 1 cup sour cream
- 3 cups beef stock
- 2 tbsp olive oil
- 2 celery stalks, chopped
- 1/2 cup mushrooms, sliced
- 1 cup grape tomatoes
- 1 cup Brussels sprouts
- Pepper
- Salt

Directions:

1. Add all ingredients except sour cream into the inner pot of instant pot and stir well.
2. Seal pot with lid and cook on high for 15 minutes.
3. Once done, release pressure using quick release. Remove lid.
4. Stir in cream and serve.

Nutritional Value (Amount per Serving):

- Calories 430
- Fat 28.1 g
- Carbohydrates 7.3 g
- Sugar 2 g
- Protein 37.3 g
- Cholesterol 127 mg

Garlic Coriander Lamb Chops

Preparation Time: 10 minutes

Cooking Time: 30 minutes

Serve: 4

Ingredients:

- 4 lamb chops
- 1 tbsp cilantro, chopped
- 1 cup beef stock
- 1/2 tsp ground coriander
- 1 tsp chili powder
- 1 tsp turmeric powder
- 1 tbsp garlic, minced
- 2 tbsp olive oil
- Pepper
- Salt

Directions:

1. Add oil into the inner pot of instant pot and set the pot on sauté mode.
2. Add garlic, lamb chops, chili powder, and turmeric and sauté for 5 minutes.
3. Add the rest of the ingredients and stir well.
4. Seal pot with lid and cook on high for 25 minutes.
5. Once done, allow to release pressure naturally. Remove lid.
6. Serve and enjoy.

Nutritional Value (Amount per Serving):

- Calories 680
- Fat 31.3 g
- Carbohydrates 1.6 g
- Sugar 0.1 g
- Protein 92.8 g
- Cholesterol 294 mg

Chapter 11: Seafood & Fish

Simple Lemon Clams

Preparation Time: 10 minutes

Cooking Time: 10 minutes

Serve: 4

Ingredients:

- 1 lb clams, clean
- 1 tbsp fresh lemon juice
- 1 lemon zest, grated
- 1 onion, chopped
- 1/2 cup fish stock
- Pepper
- Salt

Directions:

1. Add all ingredients into the inner pot of instant pot and stir well.
2. Seal pot with lid and cook on high for 10 minutes.
3. Once done, release pressure using quick release. Remove lid.
4. Serve and enjoy.

Nutritional Value (Amount per Serving):

- Calories 76
- Fat 0.6 g
- Carbohydrates 16.4 g
- Sugar 5.4 g
- Protein 1.8 g
- Cholesterol 0 mg

Italian White Fish Fillets

Preparation Time: 10 minutes

Cooking Time: 4 minutes

Serve: 4

Ingredients:

- 4 white fish fillets, frozen
- 2 tbsp olive oil
- 1/3 cup roasted red peppers, sliced
- 2 tbsp capers
- 3/4 cup olives
- 3/4 cup cherry tomatoes
- 1/4 cup water
- 1/2 tsp salt

Directions:

1. Add water into the inner pot of instant pot then place fish fillets in the pot.
2. Pour remaining ingredients over fish fillets.
3. Seal pot with lid and cook on high for 4 minutes.
4. Once done, allow to release pressure naturally for 5 minutes then release remaining using quick release. Remove lid.
5. Serve and enjoy.

Nutritional Value (Amount per Serving):

- Calories 365
- Fat 21.4 g
- Carbohydrates 4 g
- Sugar 1.6 g
- Protein 38.4 g
- Cholesterol 119 mg

Easy Salmon Stew

Preparation Time: 10 minutes

Cooking Time: 8 minutes

Serve: 6

Ingredients:

- 2 lbs salmon fillet, cubed
- 1 onion, chopped
- 2 cups fish broth
- 1 tbsp olive oil
- Pepper
- salt

Directions:

1. Add oil into the inner pot of instant pot and set the pot on sauté mode.
2. Add onion and sauté for 2 minutes.
3. Add remaining ingredients and stir well.
4. Seal pot with lid and cook on high for 6 minutes.
5. Once done, release pressure using quick release. Remove lid.
6. Stir and serve.

Nutritional Value (Amount per Serving):

- Calories 243
- Fat 12.6 g
- Carbohydrates 0.8 g
- Sugar 0.3 g
- Protein 31 g
- Cholesterol 78 mg

Rosemary Salmon

Preparation Time: 10 minutes

Cooking Time: 3 minutes

Serve: 3

Ingredients:

- 1 lb salmon
- 1 tbsp fresh lemon juice
- 1 tbsp olive oil
- 1/2 cup cherry tomatoes, halved
- 1 fresh rosemary sprig
- 10 oz fresh asparagus, trimmed
- Pepper
- Salt

Directions:

1. Pour 1 cup of water into the instant pot then place steamer rack into the pot.
2. Place salmon on steamer rack then arrange asparagus and rosemary on top of salmon.
3. Seal pot with lid and cook on high for 3 minutes.
4. Once done, release pressure using quick release. Remove lid.
5. Transfer salmon and asparagus on a plate.
6. Add cherry tomatoes on top of salmon. Season with pepper and salt.
7. Drizzle oil and lemon juice over salmon.
8. Serve and enjoy.

Nutritional Value (Amount per Serving):

- Calories 269
- Fat 14.4 g
- Carbohydrates 5.7 g
- Sugar 2.7 g
- Protein 31.8 g
- Cholesterol 67 mg

Delicious Fish Tacos

Preparation Time: 10 minutes

Cooking Time: 8 minutes

Serve: 8

Ingredients:

- 4 tilapia fillets
- 1/4 cup fresh cilantro, chopped
- 1/4 cup fresh lime juice
- 2 tbsp paprika
- 1 tbsp olive oil
- Pepper
- Salt

Directions:

1. Pour 2 cups of water into the instant pot then place steamer rack in the pot.
2. Place fish fillets on parchment paper.
3. Season fish fillets with paprika, pepper, and salt and drizzle with oil and lime juice.
4. Fold parchment paper around the fish fillets and place them on a steamer rack in the pot.
5. Seal pot with lid and cook on high for 8 minutes.
6. Once done, release pressure using quick release. Remove lid.
7. Remove fish packet from pot and open it.
8. Shred the fish with a fork and serve.

Nutritional Value (Amount per Serving):

- Calories 67
- Fat 2.5 g
- Carbohydrates 1.1 g
- Sugar 0.2 g
- Protein 10.8 g
- Cholesterol 28 mg

Quick & Easy Shrimp

Preparation Time: 10 minutes

Cooking Time: 1 minute

Serve: 6

Directions:

- 1 3/4 lbs shrimp, frozen and deveined
- 1/2 cup fish stock
- 1/2 cup apple cider vinegar
- Pepper
- Salt

Directions:

1. Add all ingredients into the inner pot of instant pot and stir well.
2. Seal pot with lid and cook on high for 1 minute.
3. Once done, release pressure using quick release. Remove lid.
4. Stir and serve.

Nutritional Value (Amount per Serving):

- Calories 165
- Fat 2.4 g
- Carbohydrates 2.2 g
- Sugar 0.1 g
- Protein 30.6 g
- Cholesterol 279 mg

Pesto Fish Fillet

Preparation Time: 10 minutes

Cooking Time: 8 minutes

Serve: 4

Ingredients:

- 4 halibut fillets
- 1/2 cup water
- 1 tbsp lemon zest, grated
- 1 tbsp capers
- 1/2 cup basil, chopped
- 1 tbsp garlic, chopped
- 1 avocado, peeled and chopped
- Pepper
- Salt

Directions:

1. Add lemon zest, capers, basil, garlic, avocado, pepper, and salt into the blender blend until smooth.
2. Place fish fillets on aluminum foil and spread a blended mixture on fish fillets.
3. Fold foil around the fish fillets.
4. Pour water into the instant pot and place trivet in the pot.
5. Place foil fish packet on the trivet.
6. Seal pot with lid and cook on high for 8 minutes.
7. Once done, allow to release pressure naturally. Remove lid.
8. Serve and enjoy.

Nutritional Value (Amount per Serving):

- Calories 426
- Fat 16.6 g
- Carbohydrates 5.5 g
- Sugar 0.4 g
- Protein 61.8 g
- Cholesterol 93 mg

Lemoney Prawns

Preparation Time: 10 minutes

Cooking Time: 3 minutes

Serve: 2

Ingredients:

- 1/2 lb prawns
- 1/2 cup fish stock
- 1 tbsp fresh lemon juice
- 1 tbsp lemon zest, grated
- 1 tbsp olive oil
- 1 tbsp garlic, minced
- Pepper
- Salt

Directions:

1. Add all ingredients into the inner pot of instant pot and stir well.
2. Seal pot with lid and cook on high for 3 minutes.
3. Once done, release pressure using quick release. Remove lid.
4. Drain prawns and serve.

Nutritional Value (Amount per Serving):

- Calories 215
- Fat 9.5 g
- Carbohydrates 3.9 g
- Sugar 0.4 g
- Protein 27.6 g
- Cholesterol 239 mg

Delicious Lemon Butter Cod

Preparation Time: 10 minutes

Cooking Time: 8 minutes

Serve: 6

Ingredients:

- 1 1/2 lbs fresh cod fillets
- 28 oz can tomato, diced
- 1 tsp oregano
- 1 onion, sliced
- 1 lemon juice
- 3 tbsp butter
- Pepper
- Salt

Directions:

1. Add butter into the instant pot and set the pot on sauté mode.
2. Add onion and sauté for 5 minutes.
3. Add remaining ingredients and stir everything well.
4. Seal pot with lid and cook on high for 3 minutes.
5. Once done, release pressure using quick release. Remove lid.
6. Stir well and serve.

Nutritional Value (Amount per Serving):

- Calories 231
- Fat 6.9 g
- Carbohydrates 29 g
- Sugar 7.5 g
- Protein 14.7 g
- Cholesterol 51 mg

Lemon Cod Peas

Preparation Time: 10 minutes

Cooking Time: 10 minutes

Serve: 4

Ingredients:

- 1 lb cod fillets, skinless, boneless and cut into chunks
- 1 cup fish stock
- 1 tbsp fresh parsley, chopped
- 1/2 tbsp lemon juice
- 1 green chili, chopped
- 3/4 cup fresh peas
- 2 tbsp onion, chopped
- Pepper
- Salt

Directions:

1. Add all ingredients into the inner pot of instant pot and stir well.
2. Seal pot with lid and cook on high for 10 minutes.
3. Once done, release pressure using quick release. Remove lid.
4. Stir and serve.

Nutritional Value (Amount per Serving):

- Calories 128
- Fat 1.6 g
- Carbohydrates 5 g
- Sugar 2.1 g
- Protein 23.2 g
- Cholesterol 41 mg

Chapter 12: Desserts

Apple Orange Stew

Preparation Time: 10 minutes

Cooking Time: 10 minutes

Serve: 4

Ingredients:

- 4 apples, cored and cut into wedges
- 1 tsp liquid stevia
- 1/2 cup orange juice
- 1 cup apple juice
- 1 tsp vanilla

Directions:

1. Add all ingredients into the inner pot of instant pot and stir well.
2. Seal pot with lid and cook on high for 10 minutes.
3. Once done, allow to release pressure naturally for 10 minutes then release remaining using quick release. Remove lid.
4. Stir well and serve.

Nutritional Value (Amount per Serving):

- Calories 161
- Fat 0.5 g
- Carbohydrates 41.2 g
- Sugar 31.9 g
- Protein 0.9 g
- Cholesterol 0 mg

Fruit Nut Bowl

Preparation Time: 10 minutes

Cooking Time: 10 minutes

Serve: 2

Ingredients:

- 1/4 cup pecans, chopped
- 1/4 cup shredded coconut
- 1 cup of water
- 3 tbsp coconut oil
- 1/2 tsp cinnamon
- 1 pear, chopped
- 1 plum, chopped
- 2 tbsp Swerve
- 1 apple, chopped

Directions:

1. In a heat-safe dish add coconut, coconut oil, pear, apple, plum, and swerve and mix well.
2. Pour water into the instant pot then place the trivet in the pot.
3. Place dish on top of the trivet.
4. Seal pot with lid and cook on high for 10 minutes.
5. Once done, release pressure using quick release. Remove lid.
6. Remove dish from pot carefully. Top with pecans and serve.

Nutritional Value (Amount per Serving):

- Calories 338
- Fat 25.4 g
- Carbohydrates 47.2 g
- Sugar 37.6 g
- Protein 1.4 g
- Cholesterol 0 mg

Applesauce

Preparation Time: 10 minutes

Cooking Time: 1 minute

Serve: 12

Ingredients:

- 3 lbs apples, peeled, cored, and diced
- 1/3 cup apple juice
- 1/2 tsp ground cinnamon

Directions:

1. Add all ingredients into the instant pot and stir well.
2. Seal pot with lid and cook on high for 1 minute.
3. Once done, allow to release pressure naturally. Remove lid.
4. Blend apple mixture using an immersion blender until smooth.
5. Serve and enjoy.

Nutritional Value (Amount per Serving):

- Calories 32
- Fat 0.1 g
- Carbohydrates 8.6 g
- Sugar 6.5 g
- Protein 0.2 g
- Cholesterol 0 mg

Sweet Coconut Raspberries

Preparation Time: 10 minutes

Cooking Time: 2 minutes

Serve: 12

Ingredients:

- 1/2 cup dried raspberries
- 3 tbsp swerve
- 1/2 cup shredded coconut
- 1/2 cup coconut oil
- 1/2 cup coconut butter

Directions:

1. Set instant pot on sauté mode.
2. Add coconut butter into the pot and let it melt.
3. Add raspberries, coconut, oil, and swerve and stir well.
4. Seal pot with lid and cook on high for 2 minutes.
5. Once done, release pressure using quick release. Remove lid.
6. Spread berry mixture on a parchment-lined baking tray and place in the refrigerator for 3-4 hours.
7. Slice and serve.

Nutritional Value (Amount per Serving):

- Calories 101
- Fat 10.6 g
- Carbohydrates 6.2 g
- Sugar 5.1 g
- Protein 0.3 g
- Cholesterol 0 mg

Cinnamon Apple

Preparation Time: 10 minutes

Cooking Time: 20 minutes

Serve: 4

Ingredients:

- 4 apples, cored and cut into chunks
- 1/2 cup apple juice
- 1 tsp liquid stevia
- 2 tsp cinnamon

Directions:

1. Add all ingredients into the instant pot and stir well.
2. Seal pot with lid and cook on low pressure for 20 minutes.
3. Once done, release pressure using quick release. Remove lid.
4. Serve and enjoy.

Nutritional Value (Amount per Serving):

- Calories 133
- Fat 0.5 g
- Carbohydrates 35.2 g
- Sugar 26.2 g
- Protein 0.7 g
- Cholesterol 0 mg

Chocolate Rice

Preparation Time: 10 minutes

Cooking Time: 20 minutes

Serve: 4

Ingredients:

- 1 cup of rice
- 1 tbsp cocoa powder
- 2 tbsp maple syrup
- 2 cups almond milk

Directions:

1. Add all ingredients into the inner pot of instant pot and stir well.
2. Seal pot with lid and cook on high for 20 minutes.
3. Once done, allow to release pressure naturally for 10 minutes then release remaining using quick release. Remove lid.
4. Stir and serve.

Nutritional Value (Amount per Serving):

- Calories 474
- Fat 29.1 g
- Carbohydrates 51.1 g
- Sugar 10 g
- Protein 6.3 g
- Cholesterol 0 mg

Choco Rice Pudding

Preparation Time: 10 minutes

Cooking Time: 20 minutes

Serve: 4

Ingredients:

- 1 1/4 cup rice
- 1/4 cup dark chocolate, chopped
- 1 tsp vanilla
- 1/3 cup coconut butter
- 1 tsp liquid stevia
- 2 1/2 cups almond milk

Directions:

1. Add all ingredients into the inner pot of instant pot and stir well.
2. Seal pot with lid and cook on high for 20 minutes.
3. Once done, allow to release pressure naturally. Remove lid.
4. Stir well and serve.

Nutritional Value (Amount per Serving):

- Calories 632
- Fat 39.9 g
- Carbohydrates 63.5 g
- Sugar 12.5 g
- Protein 8.6 g
- Cholesterol 2 mg

Chocolate Nut Spread

Preparation Time: 10 minutes

Cooking Time: 10 minutes

Serve: 4

Ingredients:

- 1/4 cup unsweetened cocoa powder
- 1/4 tsp nutmeg
- 1 tsp vanilla
- 1/4 cup coconut oil
- 1 tsp liquid stevia
- 1/4 cup coconut cream
- 3 tbsp walnuts
- 1 cup almonds

Directions:

1. Add walnut and almonds into the food processor and process until smooth.
2. Add oil and process for 1 minute. Transfer to the bowl and stir in vanilla, nutmeg, and liquid stevia.
3. Add coconut cream into the instant pot and set the pot on sauté mode.
4. Add almond mixture and cocoa powder and stir well and cook for 5 minutes.
5. Pour into the container and store it in the refrigerator for 30 minutes.
6. Serve and enjoy.

Nutritional Value (Amount per Serving):

- Calories 342
- Fat 33.3 g
- Carbohydrates 9.6 g
- Sugar 1.8 g
- Protein 7.8 g
- Cholesterol 0 mg

Spiced Pear Sauce

Preparation Time: 10 minutes

Cooking Time: 6 hours

Serve: 12

Ingredients:

- 8 pears, cored and diced
- 1/2 tsp ground cinnamon
- 1/4 tsp ground nutmeg
- 1/4 tsp ground cardamom
- 1 cup of water

Directions:

1. Add all ingredients into the instant pot and stir well.
2. Seal the pot with a lid and select slow cook mode and cook on low for 6 hours.
3. Mash the sauce using potato masher.
4. Pour into the container and store it in the fridge.

Nutritional Value (Amount per Serving):

- Calories 81
- Fat 0.2 g
- Carbohydrates 21.4 g
- Sugar 13.6 g
- Protein 0.5 g
- Cholesterol 0 mg

Chunky Apple Sauce

Preparation Time: 10 minutes

Cooking Time: 12 minutes

Serve: 16

Ingredients:

- 4 apples, peeled, cored and diced
- 1 tsp vanilla
- 4 pears, diced
- 2 tbsp cinnamon
- 1/4 cup maple syrup
- 3/4 cup water

Directions:

1. Add all ingredients into the instant pot and stir well.
2. Seal pot with lid and cook on high for 12 minutes.
3. Once done, allow to release pressure naturally for 10 minutes then release remaining using quick release. Remove lid.
4. Serve and enjoy.

Nutritional Value (Amount per Serving):

- Calories 75
- Fat 0.2 g
- Carbohydrates 19.7 g
- Sugar 13.9 g
- Protein 0.4 g
- Cholesterol 0 mg

Conclusion

The Mediterranean Refresh diet is a healthy and delicious way to nurture your overall health and well-being. Filled with hundreds of tasty, easy, and healthy recipes, this Mediterranean Refresh diet cookbook is specifically designed to help you maintain a healthy lifestyle.

This extensive cookbook combines the well-known balanced Mediterranean Refresh diet for home cooks with a wide range of innovative recipes. It's never been so simple to set the table with light, refreshing Mediterranean foods. The Mediterranean Refresh Cookbook 2021 is your key to living your healthiest lifestyle yet!